"A courageous and groundbreaking effort to build a bridge between those two communities of Christians, still largely unknown to each other, where the heart of Christ burns so brightly: the evangelical and the contemplative."
The Rev. Cynthia Bourgeault, Ph.D., Episcopal priest, author and retreat leader

"In *Pilgrimage of a Soul,* Phileena Heuertz does something quite countercultural: she goes on pilgrimage to the tomb of St. James in Spain and then on sabbatical in Durham, North Carolina. However, this is a travelogue like no other. Her journey becomes ours as she accompanies us through important landmarks of the spiritual journey: awakening, darkness, transformation, union and points in-between. In doing so, she provides a wise and helpful guidebook for the spiritual life. I've heard it said that the best writing is so individual that it has a universal appeal. And Phileena's book has just that!"
Albert Haase, O.F.M., author of *Coming Home to Your True Self* and *Living the Lord's Prayer*

"Weakness, inferiority, absence and death are turned upside down in these pages, as Phileena Heuertz engages the reader's holy imagination with Christ's good gifts of strength, mutuality, presence and life. Prepare to be transformed."
Margot Starbuck, author of *The Girl in the Orange Dress* and *Unsqueezed*

"*Pilgrimage of a Soul* is a delightful book that engaged me every step of the way. I was engrossed with Phileena's journey as she entwined her personal story with the account of a pilgrimage in Spain and theological insights she gained along the way. I heartily recommend it to all who are searching for a deeper commitment to God and to the contemplative way of life."
Christine Sine, author, contemplative, activist and executive director of Mustard Seed Associates

Phileena Heuertz

Foreword by Phyllis Tickle

PILGRIMAGE OF A SOUL

Contemplative Spirituality
for the Active Life

IVP Books

An imprint of InterVarsity Press
Downers Grove, Illinois

InterVarsity Press
P.O. Box 1400, Downers Grove, IL 60515-1426
World Wide Web: www.ivpress.com
E-mail: email@ivpress.com

InterVarsity Press® is the book-publishing division of InterVarsity Christian Fellowship/USA®, a movement of students and faculty active on campus at hundreds of universities, colleges and schools of nursing in the United States of America, and a member movement of the International Fellowship of Evangelical Students. For information about local and regional activities, write Public Relations Dept., InterVarsity Christian Fellowship/USA, 6400 Schroeder Rd., P.O. Box 7895, Madison, WI 53707-7895, or visit the IVCF website at <www.intervarsity.org>.

All Scripture quotations, unless otherwise indicated, are taken from the Inclusive Bible, The First Egalitarian Translation™ Copyright © 2007 by Priests for Equality. All rights reserved.

"Poetry" translated by Alastair Reid from Selected Poems by Pablo Neruda, published by Jonathan Cape. Reprinted by permission of the Random House Group Ltd.

Lyrics to "Hey Little Girl" and "Stronger Than Death" from Kate Hurley, Sleeping When You Woke Me (Worship Circle Records, 2006), quoted by permission.

Excerpts from Moving in the Spirit by Richard J. Hauser, S.J., Copyright ©1986 by Richard J. Hauser, S.J. Paulist Press, Inc., New York/Mahwah, NJ. Reprinted by permission of Paulist Press, Inc. www.paulistpress.com

Design: Cindy Kiple
Cover image: Valentino Sani/Trevillion Images
Interior images: butterfly: Lisa Thornberg/iStockphoto
                 hiking boots: Samuel Burt/iStockphoto
Interior art: Sarah Lance

ISBN 978-0-8308-3615-4

Printed in the United States of America ∞

Library of Congress Cataloging-in-Publication Data

Heuertz, Phileena, 1973-
    Pilgrimage of a soul: contemplative spirituality for the active
life/Phileena Heuertz.
        p. cm.
    Includes bibliographical references.
    ISBN 978-0-8308-3615-4 (pbk.: alk. paper)
    1. Contemplation. I. Title.
    BV5091.C7H48 2010
    248.3'4—dc22

2010008330

P	18	17	16	15	14	13	12	11	10	9	8	7	6	5	4	3	2	1
Y	25	24	23	22	21	20	19	18	17	16	15	14	13	12	11	10

For Chris.
Thank you for believing in me. Your passionate love,
unwavering support and enduring companionship
are my greatest treasures.

And for my godchildren:
Adina, Toby, Cora, Kirby, Nevan,
Elliott, Amani, Ada

May your life's journey always be marked with freedom
to live into the fullness of who you are.
Your lives echo immense love and boundless possibilities.

CONTENTS

FOREWORD

THERE ARE SEVEN ANCIENT DISCIPLINES—more commonly referred to nowadays as the seven ancient practices—that have shaped Christianity and Christians from before the days of our very beginning. That is to say, the seven shaped, and still shape, Judaism just as they shaped the earthly life of our Lord and of the disciples from whom we received the faith.

Three of them—tithing, fasting and the sacred meal or feast—govern the work and pleasures of our bodies. The other four practices—fixed-hour prayer, the keeping of sabbath, the observance of the liturgical year and pilgrimage—monitor or sacramentalize time, that other dimension in which we live while here. Pilgrimage—the seventh and last of the ancient practices—governs and informs and, indeed, sacramentalizes the largest unit of human time—the span of one's individual life on earth.

As Phileena Heuertz makes very clear in these pages, one of the unfortunate (necessary at the time, but subsequently unfortunate) changes that the Protestant Reformation effected was the more or less active suppression of the practices. While emphasizing the keeping of the sabbath and tithing, Protestantism merely tipped its hat at fasting while energetically discouraging overmuch concern with the sacred meal or feast, the daily offices, the close observation of the liturgical year and, of course, that most dangerous discipline of all—pilgrimage.

Pilgrimage was dangerous, in the minds of early Protestant reformers, not so much for religious or spiritual reasons but for political ones: pilgrimage within the West was inevitably made to Roman Catholic sites. (There were, in point of fact, no other real options, unless one considered that Jerusalem had retained some degree of non-catholicized Christianity; but that too was a highly debatable question.) And thus it was that pilgrimage became, in many ways, the greatest victim of the new ways; formation in the faith went from lived and physically disciplined experience to reasoned and intellectualized understanding. But the times, they are a-changing . . .

. . . Or more correctly said, the times they have changed. Now younger Christians are looking at the seven ancient practices and wondering aloud whether the abnegation of them can even be justified now—wondering, aloud and in books like this one, about how we can not only return to our formational heritage, but how we can also blend that heritage with the heritage of reasoned theology and intellectual rigor that has come to us from our more recent forebears in the faith. What we get, when younger and devout Christians—of whom Phileena is most certainly one of the more articulate—ask these questions, is often startling and even agonizing.

In this particularly startling, agonizing book, Phileena explores the sacramentalization of time, drawing from her experience on pilgrimage in Spain and on sabbatical in North Carolina. But even these very special physical settings are, for Phileena and for all of us really, in some ways better understood as windows into a more interior journey—the soul's pilgrimage through time.

The special grace of the journey that Phileena leads us on in this book entails the reconciliation of each season of life with the next, and the hope that accompanies the agony we may experience as we exit one season in order to enter another. We are guided by

Phileena in this book, but she ably reminds us that in our soul's pilgrimage we are guided by one whose ways are higher than ours.

Enter gently, then, for this is a tender book, even while at the same time it is a sinewy one. There is a candor here that makes one want to whisper, and there is a vigor of faith and a determination to live *Christian*! that makes one want to shout. If anyone among us yearns to see what post-Reformation, twenty-first-\century Christianity is leading to, then let him or her follow Phileena on El Camino de Santiago in Spain and, after that, to the Rose Cottage in North Carolina.

But go easy, and follow softly, for there is much pain here as well as much glory. Five hundred years of interruption are ending and new ways are blending in with the power of old ways. What we shall be and what we shall become as a result of that reunion are whispering here.

Listen.

Listen and hear.

Phyllis Tickle

"POETRY" by Pablo Neruda

And it was at that age . . . Poetry
arrived
in search of me. I don't know, I
don't know where
it came from, from winter or a
river.
I don't know how or when,
no they were not voices, they
were not
words, nor silence,
but from a street I was
summoned,
from the branches of night,
abruptly from the others,
among violent fires
or returning alone,
there I was without a face
and it touched me.

I did not know what to say, my
mouth
had no way
with names,
my eyes were blind,
and something started in my
soul,
fever or forgotten wings,
and I made my own way,

deciphering
that fire,
and I wrote the first faint line,
faint, without substance, pure
nonsense,
pure wisdom
of someone who knows nothing,
and suddenly I saw
the heavens
unfastened
and open,
planets,
palpitating plantations,
shadow perforated,
riddled
with arrows, fire and flowers,
the winding night, the universe.

And I, infinitesimal being,
drunk with the great starry
void,
likeness, image of
mystery,
felt myself a pure part
of the abyss,
I wheeled with the stars,
my heart broke loose on the
wind.

INTRODUCTION

Darkness. If you've experienced it, you know what I'm talking about. Darkness sets in long before we're old enough to recognize it. It begins with anguish. We've been hurt, sometimes tragically, and we don't know what to do with that injury. The safest thing seems to be to hide the pain, perhaps behind a mask. We seek to be safe by any means necessary. We learn to cope. And we achieve for ourselves a form of love, security or power that the wounded part of us desperately needs. But these coping mechanisms rob us of fullness of life. To really thrive in life, our soul needs to be transformed—over and over again. This is the work of the spiritual journey. Exercising the courage to embark on the journey postures us for radical transformation.

Many of you who are reading this book are probably persons of faith. You may feel as if you've been on the spiritual journey for quite a long time. But the spiritual journey is subtly different from our faith conversion. According to Father Thomas Keating—a Cistercian monk—at the time of conversion we orient our lives by the question, "What can I do for God?"[1] Seems appropriate, right? But when we begin the spiritual journey our life is dramatically altered toward the question, "What can God do for me?" This isn't a narcissistic, exploitative question toward a disempowered God. It's the exact opposite. This is the central question of a humble person who has awakened to their true self and to the awe-inspiring adoration of an extraordinary God.[2]

One of the things we desperately need God to do for us is to transform us from what we are today into what God intends us to be. In a world where leaders of nations are making war and preparing to defend their sovereignty by proliferating nuclear bombs, where religious fundamentalists kill innocents under the guise of righteousness, and where the average American citizen contributes daily to the destruction of our ecosphere, it is clear that we are a people in need of transformation. All of us are subject to self-deception. We commit evil and call it good. We commit violence and call it social justice.

Like the blind man Bartimaeus, when we awaken to the reality of our desperate condition we can hear Jesus asking us, "What do you want me to do for you?" (Mark 10:46-52). If we surrender and cry out, "Jesus, have mercy on me!" we have begun the spiritual journey.

Whether or not we've realized it in the depths of our being yet, we are people who need to ask what God can do for us. *You* are a person who needs to ask God, "What can you do for me?" The spiritual journey invites us into the process of radical transformation, and nothing prepares us as adequately for transformation as Christian contemplation.

The Christian contemplative tradition navigates our path toward a posture of receptivity to the One who can save us from our chaos and destruction—whether that is on a small, personal and social scale or on the grand landscape of global politics. All we have to do is submit to the process. That's it. Submit. Surrender. Dare to approach God with humble adoration. But since the beginning of time, it seems that surrender is the most difficult of postures for humanity. We much prefer self-sufficiency and self-righteousness. In our attempt to "fix" ourselves, we prefer to order, direct and define our own spirituality. In contrast, contemplative spirituality carves the posture of surrender into the fabric of our being, making us most receptive to the transformation that we cannot obtain for ourselves.

This book illuminates how I stumbled into the Christian contemplative tradition and how contemplative prayer facilitated and supported a personal awakening. In these pages I attempt to map this part of my spiritual journey against the metaphor of pilgrimage, drawing narrative from an actual pilgrimage I made in Spain. Through the vulnerability of the unfolding story, this book attempts to illuminate contemplative spirituality for the active life. The "active life" is the life all of us live. We are made to work, play and be in relationship—all very concrete ways of active living. The active life is the life fully engaged and interacting with the world. But to define what is meant by "contemplative" threatens to obliterate the essence of the concept. If we approach the meaning of the contemplative life cerebrally, with the need to analyze, dissect and define, we have missed the gift altogether. The starting place for the contemplative life is surrender. We let go of being in control. We are rendered powerless. To be contemplative is a state of being, a posture more than something concrete of which to grab hold. Even the greatest of mystics tend to use elusive language to describe the contemplative life. Contemplative spirituality is experiential and intuitive. But that doesn't mean it is only for certain personality types. Contemplative spirituality is the portal to the direct life-giving presence of God. When rooted in contemplative spirituality we are more receptive and supple in the hands of God; the life of Christ flows more freely through us.

Rather than dichotomize the active life from the contemplative life—as if it were adequate to choose to live one way or another— the abundant life brings balance or union to the active and contemplative dimensions of life. If we consider the wheel as a symbol for life, contemplation will be found in the centermost axis and the active life extends out in the spokes, as all the while the wheel is turning, progressing forward.[3] But without the center axis, the spokes lose their anchor and are unable to support the forward motion of the wheel. Without the spokes, the center axis is deemed irrelevant. When we are least connected to our contemplative center, our life is most tense and chaotic. When rooted in contemplative spirituality, the active life reflects greater peace, purpose and effectiveness.

The following practices have supported the contemplative dimension of my life for the past several years:

- "Phileena Fridays"—At first I made time and space for contemplation through rest, reflection and recreation one day per week. (I owe this to my mountain friends Andy and Andrea who first suggested such a day in my life years ago.)

- Private retreats—"Phileena Fridays" morphed into regular private retreats lasting a couple of days, four times per year, when I would force myself to be alone with self and God. I was free from the external demands of others and could battle out the internal ones.

- Sabbath—Honoring a weekly sabbath by committing to do only that which rests and nurtures my soul and is a gift of self offered back to God.[4]

- Contemplative prayer—Regular centering prayer (a minimum of two twenty-minute silent prayer periods per day). Consenting to the action of God within me through centering prayer leaves no room for hiding. When we willingly abandon ourselves to God, God calls out to our deepest self and dismantles our illusions. The true self grows in knowledge, awareness and courage.[5]

Since 1995, I have been part of organizing the movement of Word Made Flesh—an international community of Christians who serve among the most vulnerable of the world's poor. We are compelled by the vulnerabilities of children of war, children with

HIV and AIDS, abandoned children, children living on the streets, women and children enslaved in the commercial sex industry, and widows abandoned by their families. As a community we enter these dark and desperate realities and surprisingly discover the reign of God. Driven by our faith, youth and idealism, we have established compassionate communities of justice in eleven cities in the Majority World. Youth, of course, lasts only for a moment; idealism in the context of poverty, injustice, oppression and violence is challenged daily. It is our faith that remains the anchor for our service.

My faith and inevitable need for spiritual formation in the context of social activism motivate the telling of my personal story. After years of laboring with my community among the world's poor, I was in need of a calm and grounded center that could withstand the buffeting of a world full of injustice and unrelenting demands. Contemplative prayer became an oasis in an active life that was becoming arid, and it taught me how "to be," how to surrender my anxieties, compulsions and the suffering of my friends into the hands of God. Contemplative prayer taught me how to find rest in God. But the grace of contemplation also eventually led me into a life-altering dark night of the soul. The experience of internal darkness and subsequent transformation has become a wellspring for my active life.

At the heart of Christian faith is the invitation to die and be reborn. During our lifetime we may be invited into a number of deaths and rebirths. The paschal mystery of Christ serves as a model for contemplative spirituality and spiritual formation: at any given point in life we may find ourselves identifying with the passion, death and resurrection of Jesus.[6] Throughout these pages I detail my experience in the paschal mystery and hope that the telling of my story might encourage you to stay true to your own journey.

This is a story of following God, losing sight of God, seeking after and ultimately being renewed by God. This is a story of prayer as a centering, tethering event—an infusion of contemplation into a lifestyle of activism. This is a recurring human story, one of death and rebirth. It is a story of how God awakens a soul to new life.

During a retreat at St. Benedict's Monastery in Snowmass, Colorado (home of Thomas Keating), I had the privilege to be drenched in the silence of God. For ten days I met with twenty-five other retreatants from all over the world. In grand silence (silence of the eyes as well as the voice) we met together seven times per day, for a total of four hours each day, to pray. We prayed a prayer of surrender beyond words, thoughts, imagination and feeling. Together we consented to the action of God within us, growing acquainted with God who is immanent as well as transcendent. But adapting this prayer posture as a way of life isn't easy. Surrender as an active ingredient of the spiritual life invites us into a rude awakening.

Father Thomas explains the complexity of the human story in our attempt to embark on the spiritual journey:

> When we are converted to a new way of life, to service or to a particular ministry, we often experience a wonderful gift of freedom and a radical change of direction. Perhaps you have made enormous sacrifices in your business or profession, maybe even in family life, to be able to begin a journey into the service of the Gospel. But watch out! All the emotional "programs for happiness," over-identification with one's group and the commentaries that reinforce our innate tendencies have sources in the unconscious as well as in the conscious. That is why St. Paul could say, "What I want to do, I don't do. And what I don't want to do I find myself doing" (Rom 7:15ff). If we don't face the consequences of unconscious motivation—through a practice or discipline that opens us to the unconscious—then that motivation will secretly influence our decisions all through our lives.[7]

We are asleep to our unconscious motivations, and these motivations mask our true self. In essence we are hiding. And the wound in our soul remains unhealed, infecting every aspect of our lives. We are so asleep to our reality that we don't know we are hiding behind the masks of our false self. In our slumber we are unable to distinguish between what is true and what is false. These masks become so familiar to us, they become a part of our very identity.

When I awakened to the presence of masks in my life, I knew not at first what was truly me and what was a false version of me. What was a mask and what was authentic, beautiful me? Only time would tell. This is a story of what is possible when we prayerfully dare to remove our masks. And Christian contemplative spirituality provides a way to make this authentic journey through life.

In the following pages we will explore seven movements of the spiritual journey. In doing so I will draw from various experiences in my life, most extensively from my first sabbatical: on pilgrimage in northern Spain and at The Center for Reconciliation at Duke Divinity School in North Carolina.

SEASONS OF UNDIVIDED ATTENTION

My husband, Chris, and I make our home in Omaha, Nebraska. In 2007, after a combined twenty-five years of service among our impoverished friends, we received the gift of sabbatical. For the first part of our sabbatical, we determined to make a historical pilgrimage that would stretch almost five hundred miles. For thirty-three days we walked the ancient path of El Camino de Santiago. The Camino is one of three primary Christian pilgrimages—Jerusalem and Rome being the other two. For nearly twelve hundred years pilgrims have made this third-most-sacred passage, whose destination is the legendary burial ground of the apostle James, the son of Zebedee, also known as James the Great.

Pilgrims across the centuries have walked the Camino, Spanish for "way," for all manner of reasons. In one way or another, most people walk it to find themselves or to find God. Curiously, by walking this historic way most are propelled further into their life-long search for both. With each passing day I awakened more and more to the gift of my life. As time progressed I came to realize that the true essence of my being is rooted in the love of God.

Pilgrimage can be understood as a long journey in search of moral significance. It is a *way* or *passage* from one point to another. Pilgrimage is a metaphor for growth and transformation. To grow is to progress from one place to another; to be transformed is to transition from one form to another; to embark on pilgrimage is to leave where one is and arrive where one is not yet.

Pilgrimage can be a metaphor for the spiritual journey. Even the transition from sleepfulness to wakefulness is a kind of passage. Whether we are walking to a holy site or being mindful of our spiritual life, in both cases we can willfully embark on the journey or not. The choice is ours: either we decide to journey in hope of growth and change or we resign to life as it is.

When made intentionally, pilgrimage offers the gifts of detach-ment from that which is unhealthy or false and reorientation toward health, wholeness and truth. The way of pilgrimage is a contemplative presence-of-being. By posturing ourselves toward contemplation, our awareness is heightened and we can more easily submit to the process of pilgrimage—progressing from one place to another and responding with grace to the world around us.

Pilgrimage speaks to both the internal and external reality of our lives. As human beings we have the capacity to engage the world in meaningful ways through our actions. We are also able to reflect on our actions. A life characterized by pilgrimage brings union to action and contemplation. With this posture, the human condition is poised to ask questions and find answers.

For the second part of our sabbatical, following the pilgrimage, Chris and I relocated to Durham, North Carolina, as visiting prac-titioners of The Center for Reconciliation. For five months we were invited to cease our normal, active lives of service and find refuge within the embrace of Duke Divinity School. This long stretch of sabbath—characterized by detachment, rest and relative stillness—was a welcome cocoon for my active self.

The "Rose Cottage" became our home away from home. This small one bedroom house provided all the comforts we would need. As the temperature turned cooler we enjoyed the fireplace and outdoor hot tub. Pine trees towered around the house, suggesting I look up and remember the One who cares deeply for me as well as for my friends suffering in a world of cruelty. The backyard, screened porch and hammock were quiet places where I could rest from all the things I had been doing for God ("What can I do for God?") and hide away with God, whom I would come to know intimately as the Lover of my soul ("What can God do for me?"). Long, lingering walks, working with my hands in the garden, visits to the seaside and delighting in music marked my days in Durham. And gracious new friends entered my life, who became welcome companions in the journey.

The purpose of sabbatical, as dictated in the Hebrew Scriptures, took on new meaning for me.[8] An ancient practice of the early nation of Israel has profound relevance for us today. After thirteen years of social activism, sabbath and sabbatical revealed themselves as crucial gifts for my spiritual journey. This season allowed me to give my undivided attention to the movements of my soul.

SEVEN MOVEMENTS

Throughout these pages we will explore the gifts of contemplative spirituality as the central anchor for the active life, service and mission. Transformation is what the spiritual journey postures us to receive and is supported by the active-contemplative continuum. Within this dynamic we find movements or rings that illuminate growth.

Awakening is the first movement in the spiritual journey. Six movements follow: longing, darkness, death, transformation, intimacy and union. Picture seven three-dimensional rings all interlocked. Each ring represents a movement or season in the soul's development. During a process of formation, the soul moves throughout these rings at various times, in no particular order. The spiritual journey is more cyclical than linear. Each moment in a certain movement or ring provides a necessary experience for personal and spiritual growth and development. At times we may progress from one ring to another, only to find ourselves revisiting a former ring for a deeper work in our ever-growing soul. The following pages attempt to bring to light these hidden mysteries and wonders of the spiritual life.

This is my story. But in many ways it is *our* story. It's a story of awakening, darkness and transformation. It's a story of being born. It's a story of striving to be free. As a Christian it is a story of ongoing transformation in the image of Christ. As a Christian *woman,* it is a story of feminine awakening as central to spiritual formation—a story that cries out to be heard by women and men alike. This is a story of questions and doubt, sorrow and grief, death and love. Embracing these realities is the essence of the spiritual journey. As you enter into my journey, let these movements burrow deep into your soul, so that your own story might emerge with more clarity.

St. Benedict's Monastery
Snowmass, Colorado
September 2009

1   AWAKENING

It is never too late to be what you might have been.

GEORGE ELIOT

WHEN I WAS A CHILD my mother would wake me in a most delightful fashion. She'd come in and draw open the shades and sing,

Good morning, good morning, good morning.
It's time to rise and shine.
Good morning, good morning, good morning.
I hope you're feeling fine.
The sun is just above the hills
and all the day's for us to fill.
The day is calling just for you
and all your dreams are coming true.

Though my husband, Chris, hasn't adopted this way of waking me, eventually I do rise and attempt to shine. Usually I rise before him anyway, though on occasion he has been known to grace me with "the morning dance." Only a few have been so lucky as to witness him strutting around like a proud peacock or "old school gangster," as he puts it. In this fashion he sets the tone for a day full of joy and laughter.

You know how it is when you wake up from a long, deep sleep? At first it's a struggle. I often find myself in this "somewhere in between" space, not quite sure where to land. Sometimes the dream I was having was so nice I want to continue it. Or at times the dream feels more real than the life waiting for me when I wake. Do you ever experience that psychological quagmire where you wonder if reality really is dreamland and what you presume to be your waking state, fantasy?

When it's time to wake up, I find myself wavering between going back into the dark state of slumber that feels comfortable and familiar, and giving in to the pull to open my eyes and transition into the realness of the day. Sleep is comforting. It rests the body and mind and, for a few hours, frees us from the stress and anxieties of life. Maybe it is the stress and anxieties that we're trying to avoid by staying in bed. Choosing to disrupt a comfortable, peaceful state of existence for the unknowns of a day that could include pain seems kind of absurd. Isn't dreamland a better place to be? But sleeping too much is a common symptom of depression. And living life perpetually asleep doesn't seem like much of a life at all. The comatose condition is nothing to be envied.

In our contemporary times, we are so busy that some of us hardly take time to sleep. With the advances of technology, life is fast and very full. Primitive times offered a much slower, calmer pace with more natural opportunities for silence and solitude, in addition to hard physical labor, which is good for the body as well as the soul. Now with electricity we are less in touch with the natural rhythms and cycles of our days, months and years. We can stay up as late as we want with the aid and company of light bulbs, television, DVDs, iPhones, Xbox, Facebook and Twitter. If societies that came before us could see us, they might think we were a bunch of overactive crazies.

Cloaked by overactivity, a typical day in the life of many of us is marked with avoidance and escape. Busyness sometimes serves to help us evade the vulnerable places in our hearts that are wounded and afraid. Perhaps we numb the pain within by filling our lives with commotion and workaholism, we create a full social life to avoid the interior life, or we try to dull the ache by eating, drinking or exercising too much. Others do the opposite—in an attempt to avoid pain they suppress or control it by not eating and by other repressive behaviors. Indulgences of most kinds are often signs that we are avoiding or trying to escape our pain.

Sometimes we resist retiring for the day because it is on our bed at night that everything stops and we can no longer escape the voices in our head or the ache in our heart. The stillness and silence of bedtime is sometimes haunting rather than peace-filled. When we've used so much energy to try to avoid our personal turmoil, and we finally manage to reach dreamland, why would we want to wake up? Another day sometimes threatens us with more avoidance and sedation. And so the cycle continues: we live our days finding ways to sedate our woundedness and, if we're lucky, we find an escape at night through sleep. Inevitably, though, it will be time to wake once again from our slumber and attempt to live the chaos of another day. Day after day the morning comes and the gift of the hours is ours to receive. So we rise. After all, we do have a life to live. And if we remain in a state of perpetual sleep we might as well be dead.

WAKING UP IN ST. JEAN PIED DE PORT

It was a brisk, springtime morning in St. Jean Pied de Port, France. The sun had yet to rise on the foothills of the Pyrenees Mountains. The birds hadn't even begun singing their morning songs. But the promises of pilgrimage stirred in our hearts as we forced our eyes open and stumbled out of bed. El Camino de Santiago stretched out before us and summoned us to our feet. It wasn't long after leaving our guesthouse that we spotted the first yellow arrow to direct our way. All along the Camino yellow arrows mark the path—painted on trees, rocks, streets and buildings. Whether we walked on dirt paths, gravel roads or village streets, the arrows guided our way.

The long flight from Omaha to Chicago to Bilbao in the Spanish Basque region, followed by the winding train that marked the entrance into our journey, culminated on that morning. After decades of service among our impoverished friends, Chris and I detached from our work and determined to walk the ancient Camino.

Just before setting out on our first day's journey we read the following reflection as a prayer for pilgrimage:

> Up early on this first day and not at all sure you want to embark on a journey to some distant, fabled place. Why bother? You would prefer to be asleep, warm within the comfort of your day-to-day routines.
>
> Yet you start on your pilgrimage, unsure of what lies ahead or even why you've chosen to go on such an arduous adventure. You only hope that, drawn forward by the lure of some far-off sacred city, you will find journey's end worth the hardships along the way.
>
> At the same time, you sense a call to some larger purpose, a call that will not be denied.
>
> Knowing that the road flows forward beyond your time of pilgrimage, just as it winds behind you through countless other lifetimes, fills you with a sense that you are part of a great continuum.
>
> You take a deep breath, put your pack on your shoulders, and step out onto the road.[1]

The spiritual journey too is marked with an invitation to wake up. The Buddha is remembered to have said that people live most of their life asleep.[2] Of course he didn't mean that people spend most of their lives in bed, physically asleep. Five hundred years before the time of Christ, the Buddha referenced the spiritual condition of humanity. Jesus echoed this universal truth when he said, "I came that you might have life and have it to the full" (John 10:10)—in contrast to a "partial" life. The Christian journey begins with an invitation to wake from our sleepfulness. As St. Irenaeus said, "The glory of God is a human being fully alive." It's hard to be fully alive if we stay asleep. By waking up, we determine to embark on the spiritual journey.

Like my mother's morning ritual or my husband's dance, there are spiritual practices that can help us wake up and fully live. The posture of pilgrimage and the practice of contemplative prayer have been vital to my awakening. As I have awakened, I've endured brokenness, confronted the false self and experienced new revelation of the love of God. Awakening is difficult and life altering, but the glory of God compels nothing less.

BROKENNESS

Months prior to setting out on the Camino, I had a sense that I would not be the same when I returned. In a state of awakening, my identity was being shaken and dismantled, and I was entering an internal nakedness. It's difficult to describe this experience. Only in hindsight can I really name it for what it was. I felt like I was losing my orientation for life, relationships and service. During prayer I would often find myself in tears and not know why. (This is an outward sign of what Thomas Keating calls "divine therapy.") I found myself needing to differentiate in new ways from my husband, my community and my work. But that left me feeling very insecure with seemingly no anchor to keep me stabilized. Jesus points to this transformation when he says, "He who seeks only himself brings himself to ruin, whereas he who brings himself to nothing for my sake discovers who he is" (Matthew 10:39 NAB).[3]

In this internally exposed condition I felt vulnerable, insecure and fragile. Symbolized by pilgrimage but realized through awakening, I was finding out that I wasn't who I thought I was. Meet the false self—the shadow of who we truly are, the expression of who we are that pales in comparison to the truth of who we were created to be. The false self is so much a part of our identity that we don't know it is there. We don't distinguish it from our true self.

St. Paul taught about the false self and true self using the language of "old and new creation" in 2 Corinthians. "Therefore, if anyone is in Christ, [she] is a new creation; the old has gone, the new has come!" (2 Corinthians 5:17 NIV). He also described the battle between the two in the process of being transformed into the likeness of Christ. "I don't understand what I do—for I don't do the things I want to do, but rather the things I hate. . . . This makes me the prisoner of the law of sin in my members" (Romans 7:15, 23).

Watchman Nee, the famous Chinese Christian author and church leader of the early twentieth century, expanded on this teaching and spoke of the "old man" and the "new man." Thomas Merton, Trappist monk, spiritual writer, poet and social activist, wrote of this ideology as the "false self" and "true self." Mystics throughout the ages have spoken and written prolifically on this state of our human condition.

The apostle Paul explains in Ephesians the spiritual revolution that we need in order to grow into the life of Christ or our true self.

So I declare and testify together with Christ that you must stop living the kind of life the world lives. Their minds are empty, they are alienated from the life of God. . . . That is hardly the way you have learned from Christ, unless you failed to hear properly, when you were taught what the truth is in Jesus. You must give up your old way of life; you must put aside your old self, which is being corrupted by following illusory desires. Your mind must be renewed by a spiritual revolution, so that you can put on the new self that has been created in God's likeness, in the justice and holiness of the truth. (Ephesians 4:17-18, 20-24)

Awakening and embarking on the spiritual journey invited me to have a good hard look at reality. I was being invited to die so that more of the life of Christ could live in me. "For to me to live is Christ and to die is gain" (Philippians 1:21).

In those moments, days and months I began to recognize my false self and the ways in which it controlled me and kept me from being fully alive. "False Phileena" let particular cultural and religious expectations define and limit her. I was overly concerned with what others thought of me, and those actual or delusional opinions determined many of the decisions I made and responsibilities I stepped up to. My true self was a "prisoner of the law of sin at work within me." But having embarked on the spiritual journey, my true self was waking up and was a force to be reckoned with.

Reflecting on the gospel message, Thomas Keating says that the first stage of the spiritual journey involves the dismantling of one's worldview and self-image.[4] Over time, I began to distinguish the false self from the true. This is nothing short of a profound grace, for we cannot make ourselves grow. We can only will to wake up and submit to the process.

Waking up and embarking on this journey involved an uprooting and tearing down of my false self and worldview. At times I felt like I was coming undone. Submission to this grace reoriented my life to a deeper degree of truth. The transformative work of Christ is very real. By a mystery that can hardly be explained, the work of Christ sets us free. The true self is free once the false self is confronted and dismantled.

This is Jesus' promise to us—that it would be "no longer I who live but Christ who lives in me" (Galatians 2:20). The false self has to "die" in order for Christ's life to reign in us. This is the spiritual journey—to live into the fullness of Christ's life within us.

But living into our potential is not easy.

All sorts of factors inhibit us from reaching our full potential and divert us instead toward the reinforcement of a false self. For many women, one big factor is patriarchy. Men too report awakening to perils of male domination. Various sectors of society, in both subtle and painfully conspicuous ways, effectively repress the feminine. Male and female alike suffer from this repression.

SUBJUGATION OR MUTUALITY?

Central to my awakening and growth was the breaking or dismantling of patriarchal paradigms that had stifled me from reaching my full potential and had contributed to the creation of the false self. Slowly I began to recognize the effect of patriarchy (male dominance and superiority) on culture, religion, family and my personal life. Rising from my slumber meant examining all sectors of society that repress the feminine. Power and powerlessness were constant companions in this awakening. Power paradigms that communicate a "woman's place" in a limiting and repressive manner came into view. I felt powerless and longed to be empowered.

Awakening invited me to be broken of who I thought I was (the false self) and to submit to the work of the Spirit in me, which enabled me to submit to who I truly was (the true self). Even submission started to take on new meaning. Submission as mutuality was making sense to me, instead of submission as subordination or subjugation. Mutuality is love-reciprocated submission. This was good news to me.

Growing up, the typical model of male-female relationships that I witnessed looked something like this: In church, only the man was allowed to teach from the holy pulpit. Women were not permitted to teach men. Women weren't allowed to pass the offering plate or to serve Communion either. They were consigned to playing the piano, singing in the choir, teaching women and children, and cooking and serving church dinners. And the more revered women became missionaries in faraway places where they could minister more freely (somewhere else).

Though my dad was supportive of my mom and me pursuing our dreams, many of the marriages I witnessed took on this kind of expression: The husband always had to drive the car, even if the wife wanted to. The husband also expected dinner to be made by a certain time and his laundry to be washed. The wife was expected to meet every need of her husband. And if the husband committed an affair, social gossip usually indicted the wife for not being attentive enough to her husband's sex drive.

The woman wasn't even afforded a name of her own. She belonged to her father and then to her husband, most well-noted through her last name. And a woman was subtly defined in relationship to men through her title as Miss, Ms. or Mrs. Obviously, a man is not subjected to such definitions: he is Mr. no matter his marital status.

My mom was one of the more radical women of her day. She is spunky, intelligent and courageous. Raised by her widowed mother, Mom witnessed daily as a child, adolescent and young adult how a woman can be independent, free-thinking, creative and a provider for her family. Throughout her life, Mom could often be found breaking with convention, much to the dismay and ridicule of others. She was the first preacher's wife to wear pants to the church in which I grew up—a subversive act indeed.[5] I remember her telling me this story and how she thought the whole congregation would be scandalized. But it wasn't long before several of the women quietly thanked her and told how they had wanted to be free to wear pants instead of skirts or dresses to church (especially in winter). Though Mom often resisted the status quo, she couldn't escape all the influence of patriarchy. Bright, talented and hardworking, she worked an average of thirty-five hours per week to put herself through college. But Mom did what many women in her day did—she discontinued her college education once she married. She used to joke about getting her "M-R-S degree." In fact, many women in her generation were noted for such an accomplishment. Even twenty years later at the college I graduated from, this tradition was evident. My peers and I witnessed the same phenomenon— women attending class and receiving education but aspiring to their "M-R-S degrees."

To a young girl trying to find her way in the world, the message was clear. Not only am I defined in relationship to my husband and subjugated to him, but my opportunities are limited by him. This message was subtly engraved into my very being, taking shape in the following mental musing.

> You can be anything you want to be in life except a pastor, elder or deacon. Why? Because you are female. You are less. You are a little lower than your male counterpart. Because of no reason other than your gender, you are to submit to male authority. You can attend church and maybe help out in the nursery, but you have nothing worthwhile to share in the company of men, except service of their needs and the feeding of their ego. Though you can be anything you want to be except a leader of men, your highest calling is that of wife and mother, so be satisfied with that alone. And once you obtain this most worthy of callings, your duty as wife and mother is to please your husband and care for your children. Serve your husband and support him and your children even if it means repressing your own dreams. Your identity is found in relationship to your husband and children.

Many of the predominant people in my life as a child, teen and young adult viewed a woman's place in life as reflected in Debi Pearl's book *Created to Be His Help Meet*. Pearl is cofounder with her husband of "No Greater Joy Ministries" and coauthor of the book *To Train Up a Child*. In *Created to Be His Help Meet*, Pearl gives women advice about how to be a godly woman, wife and mother. She sums up well the patriarchal teaching by which I was conditioned. While this view has left the mainstream, it can still be found in understated forms, and its impact on both women and men extends well beyond the fundamentalist churches that will preach it.

In essence Pearl suggests that being a woman is defined by one's role as wife and mother—it is her "created nature."[6] "A good help meet will have a passion to be of service. Her first calling is to be of service to her husband, then her children, and when time affords, her passion of service will spill over to serving others."[7]

At one point early in the book Pearl responds to a woman who sought her advice about her husband's emotional affair with his secretary. In shocking rhetoric that has been widely accepted in Christian circles, Pearl instructs this woman and all those reading her book to exploit her beauty and sexuality and compete with the secretary in order to win her husband's affection and fidelity. "God has provided for your husband's complete satisfaction and deliverance from temptation through you. . . . Your man, like many men before him, is a fool to wink at sin, to play with temptation."[8]

Pearl goes on to explain that, if the woman confronts her husband, calls him to account and asks him to change his behavior, the marriage will end in divorce. She'll be standing on principle, Pearl says, but she'll be sleeping alone. And if she finds another husband, Pearl says, he'll be no better than her first.

> Get down on your husband's emotional level, and make yourself more attractive than that office wench, and do it to-day! . . . Never demand that a man love you and cherish you because he ought to. Earn every smile and shared moment. Cultivate his love for you. . . . Be creative and aggressive in your private, intimate times. Keep him drained at home so he won't have any sexual need at work. If you feed him well, emotionally and sexually, her cooking won't tempt him.[9]

As I reviewed Debi Pearl's book, which was being read by a number of our friends, I couldn't believe the blatant female subordina-

tion and male domination she promotes. Pearl sums up her perception of the biblical mandate of female subjugation by saying,

> There is no loss of dignity in subordination when it serves a
> higher purpose. God made you to be a help meet to your
> husband so you can bolster him, making him more produc-
> tive and efficient at whatever he chooses to do. You are not
> on the board of directors with an equal vote. You have no
> authority to set the agenda. But if he can trust you, he will
> make you his closest advisor, his confidant, his press secre-
> tary, his head of state, his vice-president, his ambassador,
> his public relations expert, maybe even his speech writer—
> all at his discretion.[10]

This kind of submission is a picture of power and powerlessness, exploiter and exploited, superiority and inferiority, better
and less. Women are not lovable and lovely in and of themselves;
they must "earn" the love of others. Submission of this nature is
the result of a power paradigm that favors men. Women are created for and expected to serve the sole benefit of men. When
women adhere to this view, they are held captive from reaching
their potential.

One would think this book was published in the 1950s, but
make no mistake—it was published in 2004. This kind of manipulation and self-exploitation disguised as "submission" and "godly"
is a widely accepted posture for many women.

In stark contrast to Pearl's perspective, on the Camino I grew
aware of a different kind of submission. Chris and I each encountered physical, mental and emotional obstacles that we had never
experienced before. At times, I needed Chris to support me and
keep me going. At other times Chris needed me to support and
encourage him. Mutuality. The presumption I had grown up
under—that the woman submits to the man as part of the natural
order of things, that to submit means to suppress myself and ele-

vate someone else, not as an act of mercy but as an act of penance for my gender—was being subverted and reshaped as we made our way together along the Camino. We needed one another, and we needed to trust one another.

Mutuality is beautifully expressed in John 13. In this passage we learn of the Last Supper—Jesus' last Passover meal with his disciples before he was crucified. With a totally countercultural gesture Jesus insisted on washing his friends' feet. Here the teacher stooped down to do the job of a slave. One of the disciples, Peter, was indignant and initially refused to let Jesus touch his grimy, first-century feet. But Jesus told Peter that unless he allowed Jesus to do this, Peter would have no part in him. Peter's response was then one of total submission. He asked Jesus to not stop with his feet but to wash his hands and head as well.

Peter's initial reaction to Jesus is similar to our gut reaction. We don't want Jesus to "go there"—to those vulnerable, needy places in us. We want to pretend that we are self-sufficient, capable people who don't need anything from anyone. Peter's submission to Jesus required Peter's own admittance of his weakness, his need. The act of Jesus washing his feet would expose Peter's vulnerability. Submission is about receiving, but sadly society and culture have made it about subjugation. And so a power paradigm is created in which often women are expected to "submit" (subjugate themselves) and men don't posture themselves to receive (submit).

Unfortunately, a lot of Christian women have embraced the posture of "submission" (subjugation) to their detriment. One way this subjugated posture is often endured is by pretending that we as women don't need anything. We can do it all and ask for nothing in return—run the household; birth and nurse the babies; feed, care for and support the husband; maybe work a job to help meet the financial needs of the family; and, if there's time left over, serve in the church, most likely in the nursery. In a world where the woman is intricately connected and subjected to the needs of everyone around her, there is no room for dreams of her own. She exists for everyone else. And she can continue to live that way if she pretends she is not vulnerable and needy herself. Once she admits her own need (to dream, perhaps, and to give expression to those dreams and ambitions), the natural order of family and societal dynamics is thunderously shaken.

In contrast, mutual submission between men and women invites us into true intimacy and frees us to give as well as receive and to live into our full potential. Mutuality between anyone, regardless of gender, is redemptive.

At the church I'm a part of today, Jesuit priests courageously demonstrate the lesson Jesus taught Peter in a foot-washing ceremony on Holy Thursday. With a humility rarely demonstrated by the powerful, these brilliant, dignified men humble themselves in a posture of receptivity and let others wash their feet. In so doing they reveal a central characteristic of an apostle of Christ—vulnerability.

The ones who hold power in any institution are often the most guarded—they are glad for others to reveal their hidden vulnerabilities and needs, but they neglect to reveal their own need. Meeting the needs of someone else may be kind, compassionate and even righteous, but it is, after all, a powerful gesture: *You have a need, and I can meet that need. You need me, but I don't need you.* The reverse is in view during the Holy Thursday ceremony. This isn't an exhibition of the powerful doing something for the needy, but an expression of our common humanity, with the capacity to give and the need to receive. Parishioners are invited to participate as well—parishioners and priests, men and women, giving and receiving with mutual respect. The point of the service is to remember the gift of mutuality—that we need one another, that we are not self-sufficient and that while we do have a lot to offer and give, we also have need to receive. During this grace-filled church service wounds and needs are embraced as avenues for mutual grace and transformation.

Waking up caused my worldview of submission to be shattered, breaking along with it my inferior and subordinate view of self. This was a rather new way of understanding brokenness. Often I had associated the need for brokenness with the sin of pride. Strangely, the brokenness invitation I received was one of being broken of self-abnegation or self-effacing. I was like the woman in the Gospel of St. Luke who was bent over for eighteen years by an evil spirit—Jesus' healing of her meant a strengthening of her spine to stand up straight. She didn't need to be broken of pride but to be broken of what shackled her in a posture of oppression.[11]

The invitation during this season of awakening was "self-assertion"—to be broken free of what was holding me back from being more truly and fully me and to stand up straight with proper confidence. Marianne Williamson articulates the fears we encounter upon awakening:

> "Our deepest fear is not that we are inadequate. Our deepest fear is that we are powerful beyond measure. It is our light, not our darkness that most frightens us." We ask ourselves, Who am I to be brilliant, gorgeous, talented, fabulous? Actually, who are you *not* to be? You are a child of God. Your playing small does not serve the world. There is nothing enlightened about shrinking so that other people won't feel insecure around you. We are all meant to shine, as children do. We were born to make manifest the glory of God that is within us. It's not just in some of us; it's in everyone. And as we let our own light shine, we unconsciously give other people permission to do the same. As we are liberated from our own fear, our presence automatically liberates others.[12]

Waking up allowed me to surrender to the removal of masks of fear, inferiority and subordination. I was coming out from hiding and breaking free of that which kept me from being fully awake, fully alive. Some of what I needed to be liberated from was familial, cultural and religious paradigms of what it means to be a woman. I began realizing just how much I was living my life for other people rather than for who God made me to be. I was realizing how much I put everyone else first like a good self-denying Christian, only to discover how in some of those ways I was *hiding* and pretending that I didn't have needs and dreams. The easier, *broader* way was to hide behind selfless deeds rather than to live up to my potential to influence and to create change, to heal and to lead.

Theologians Reinhold Niebuhr and Carol Lakey Hess help me understand this notion of *hiding* as the sin of self-abnegation, the cousin sin of pride.[13] According to a number of theologians, the sin of self-abnegation is widely overlooked in Christian teaching, yet it has as devastating effects on people and society as does the sin of pride.

Niebuhr suggested that sin takes on two primary expressions. The first is "the unwillingness of [humanity] to acknowledge [their] creatureliness and dependence upon God and [their] effort to make [their] own life independent and secure," which is commonly understood as pride.[14] The alternative form of sin is sensuality (doing what feels good), evasion of self or self-abnegation. Unfortunately, Niebuhr underdeveloped this side and focused most of his work on the first expression of sin. Both expressions are effectively a form of denial. Pride is *the denial of one's need to depend* on God; self-abnegation is *the knowledge of the need but refusal to depend* on God. Pride can be associated with a superiority complex; self-abnegation can be associated with an inferiority complex. Both prevent us from living into the fullness of who God created us to be.

I think of Moses as a good example of one who struggled with self-abnegation. In the Torah, Exodus 3–4 outlines this marvelous story. God calls Moses to lead the Hebrew people out of slavery, but Moses doubts his abilities and tries to wiggle out of the calling. The Scriptures mention four times that Moses responds to God with "what ifs" and excuses. Self-abnegation is seen clearly in Exodus 4:10-14. Moses understands that in order for the people to be liberated, he will have to speak to the king of Egypt to negotiate their release—a tall order, no doubt. Moses seems afraid and doubtful that this is going to work. By way of struggling with the calling and delaying to step up to the responsibility, Moses says that he is not a good speaker:

> Then Moses said to the Holy One, "Please, my God, I am not good with words. I wasn't yesterday, nor the day before, nor am I now, even after you spoke to me. I speak slowly, and with a wooden tongue."
>
> YHWH replied, "Who taught people to speak in the first place? Who makes them deaf or mute? Who makes them see, or be blind? Who, if not I, YHWH? Now go! I myself will be with you when you speak. I will teach you what to say."
>
> But Moses said, "Please, my God, please send someone else. Not me."
>
> Then God's anger flashed out against Moses. "If you can't do it, I know someone who can."

How many times have we been like Moses—full of self-doubt and reluctant to step into our calling? Self-abnegation and sensuality are intricately connected, but at first it is difficult to recognize the connection. Often, doing what feels good (sensuality) means hiding or avoiding one's potential. When we are subject to the sin of self-abnegation, we are shirking our responsibilities. Fear is usually a contributor. We fear upsetting the status quo or we fear our abilities or we fear the potential for rejection, criticism and failure—so we hide. Hiding feels safe.

With the support of a number of scholars, feminist theologian Judith Plaskow explains the problematic nature of overemphasizing the sin of pride while neglecting the sin of self-abnegation. Carol Lakey Hess summarizes Plaskow's point by saying that a description of "sin as self-assertion, self-centeredness, and pride

speaks out of and to the experience of powerful men. . . .
[W]omen are better indicted for such behaviors as lack of self,
self-abnegation, and irresponsibility"—the alternative expression of sin that Niebuhr recognized. "When sin as pride is gener-
alized, self-abnegation is deemed a virtue and harmfully reinforced" in the lives of the historically powerless. "A theology that
emphasizes self-sacrifice as the human telos functions to further
enervate women's struggle for self-assertion. Such a theology may
chasten little boys, but hasten the devastation of girls."[15]

In this movement of my soul, I was waking up to the fullness of
being created in the image of God—male *and* female God created
them. There was something beautiful and divine to be embraced in
my feminine identity. I was confronting the sin of self-abnegation
and growing in self-assertion rooted in dependence on God. Sadly,
a theology that overemphasized self-sacrifice had served to devas-
tate me. Now awakened, I realized that spiritual growth for me
meant owning the responsibility to live into my potential to offer
my voice, perspective and influence—at the risk of upsetting the
status quo and being criticized and rejected. Once awakened, I
couldn't turn back. Pilgrimage is not a round trip. The spiritual
journey beckoned me further and deeper into the consequences of
patriarchal theology and practice.

THE LOVE OF GOD

In her album *Sleeping When You Woke Me,* Kate Hurley beautifully
echoes the process of awakening through song. In the track "Hey
Little Girl," we hear of a small child and the root of her pain. The
pain inflicted at a young age is too much to bear. It is deeper than
even tears can express. The child grows up to be a woman only to
find that the "little girl" is still within her:

I see a little girl
In the back of my mind

See daisies in her hand
She's looking to the sky
She is looking to the sky
She is sitting on the stairs
Of her two story house
And the pain that she bears
Leaves no tears left to cry
Leaves her no tears left to cry
Where is the reward
For the ones who have been torn
Where is the treasure laid for the
Ones who've known so much pain

Hey little girl
Let me whisper some hope
There's mercy for you that overflows
Everything's going to be all right
Everything's going to be all right
Hey little girl won't you hear me say
There is love enough
To cover your shame
Everything's going to be all right
Everything's going to be all right

And that little girl
So small and so scared
Been near so long
I forgot she was there
I forgot that she was there
Somehow the pain
That she couldn't feel
Passed on to me
A weight too great to bear
Much too great to bear

Someone is standing near
Who will wash away her tears
Someday when she's been found
Her scars will become a crown.[16]

My initial awakening could probably be traced back two or three years before I made pilgrimage in Spain. I had decided to make regular private retreats, and my first was a day spent at the Abbey of Gethsemani in Trappist, Kentucky—former home of Thomas Merton. This was my introduction to the prophetic presence of monastic communities. In the monks' silence, I encountered the penetrating presence of God.

What started out as a few silent retreat days per year turned into a quarterly rhythm of overnight private retreats. Though there are many places that have provided solitude and silence for me, one of my favorites and the place I most regularly return to is a small Benedictine monastery in rural Schuyler, Nebraska.

During one of my visits to Schuyler, Kate's song wakened me to some of the pain in my heart that I had previously been numb to. Her song gave rise to haunting questions and painful doubts within me. I found myself asking, *What is this pain that I feel? Why am I so sad? Who is this little girl in me and what is her pain?*

The descent continued. Questions ran deep as I sat in my little cell at the monastery and cried and cried until I thought I could cry no more. Tears gave rise to words: *Who am I really? Am I lovely? Am I loved? Am I really loved for me? Does anyone see me? Does anyone know that I'm alive? Does anyone care? I have dreams to dream! I have a life to live! Does anyone hear me? Does anyone see me?*

The root of all these questions was an invitation to realize to a deeper degree of faith that God loves me, truly loves me. Thankfully, I grew up in a Christian home where my parents did everything they could to communicate to me the love of God. For the daughter of a pastor who grew up attending church three times a week, this was Sunday school lesson 101: "For God so loved the world, that he gave his only begotten Son, that whosoever believeth in him should not perish, but have everlasting life" (John 3:16 KJV). However, the "love" message got somewhat lost amidst the fear of "perishing." Subtly, the idea that I could do something to avoid perishing became a primary unconscious motivator in my life. Rather than letting the love message sink in, the louder message I absorbed was how to avoid being punished and damned to hell. "God loved the world so much that God sacrificed the Son to save us from hell" didn't get through to me that well. Certainly over time I grew to want to be in relationship with my Creator and with the one who I was told expressed this earth-shattering act of love for me through a crucifixion. But recognizing, realizing and experiencing the *love* of God seemed to evade me. The sentiment that we are "sinners in the hands of an angry God" seemed to subtly underline a lot of the "Christian" teaching I received.

This is simply (or complexly, depending on how you look at it) the human condition that we're all faced with if we awaken to it. We are cut off from our Creator—the one who provides our every need—and we spend our lives trying to return to and live in that all-fulfilling relationship. We long for the Garden—the place that symbolizes the relationship between God and humanity. In the Garden all is right with the world. The true self is free to be expressed in her fullness. Men and women live together in life-giving mutuality. But the sins of self-abnegation and pride ruin this utopia. We are cut off, fragmented, distanced from God and from one another. It is easier to remain asleep to this reality because it can be downright traumatizing to wake up.

Ironically, in the garden story of the Hebrew Scriptures it seems that Adam is the one who fell to the sin of self-abnegation, while Eve succumbed to the sin of pride. When Eve submitted to the temptation to become like God, she sinned by exhibiting "an unwillingness to acknowledge [her] creatureliness and dependence

upon God and [her] effort [was] to make [her] own life independent and secure"; while Adam in contrast exhibited sensuality and
evasion of self, the sin of self-abnegation.[17] When God asked Adam
why he did that which God had told him not to do, he replied, "It
was the woman you put beside me, she gave me the fruit, and I ate
it" (Genesis 3:12). A little speculation causes me to conclude that
either Adam thought the fruit looked good (sensuality) or he didn't
think for himself (evasion of self). Either way, the sin of self-
abnegation seems clear. Interestingly, one of the consequences of
Adam and Eve's sin would be a lack of mutuality and union between men and women. "You will desire union with your man, but
he will be bent on subjugating you" (Genesis 3:16).

In our feeble attempts to return to the Garden—which represents union with God and mutuality among humanity—we either
appeal to substitutes or we respond to the world in an exploitative
manner to get the power and control, affection and esteem, or security and survival that we crave.

Thomas Keating writes and speaks copiously about our es-
trangement from God. A doctor of psychology and theology, he
examines what it means to be human in a holistic way. By understanding the depths of the mind, will and emotions Keating is able
to connect the teachings of Christ with the most vulnerable parts
of our human condition. In his book *The Human Condition: Contemplation and Transformation,* he outlines three basic "programs
for happiness," of which he says that each of us usually over-
identifies with one:

- power and control

- affection and esteem

- security and survival

These "programs for happiness" invariably conflict with one
another so that the space between us becomes toxic. None of our
relationships "outside of the Garden" will offer us power and

control, affection and esteem, and security and survival to the extent that we need.

Keating says that these three "programs for happiness" emerge from very basic instinctual needs. It is a natural part of our human development to seek a degree of power and control, affection and esteem, and security and survival. The problem is that in time we over-identify with one set by way of compensating for that basic need which may have gone largely unmet in our childhood; thus, the false self gains fuel for its existence. This intensifies when we over-identify with a particular group or culture. Temperament also plays into the false self. For example, if I am a dominant personality type and I didn't experience the control that I needed as a child, I will be compelled to control my situation and surroundings and in some cases other people. Experiencing anxiety and frustration is often a sign that in the unconscious there is an emotional program for happiness that has just been triggered.[18] Do you ever have an overly emotional reaction to a situation or relationship and later wonder why you reacted so strongly? As we grow in self-awareness we often realize that some of our reactions to present circumstances are actually reactions to past events that are buried in our unconscious. The current situation provides a trigger for the unresolved anguish. When we recognize the agony surfacing, we have experienced grace. This is an invitation to greater wholeness.

"The spiritual journey is a journey of self-discovery since the encounter with God is also an encounter with one's deepest self," says Keating.[19] Thomas Merton spoke of "finding [oneself] in God" and wrote, "In order to find God, Whom we can only find in and through the depths of our own soul, we must therefore first find ourselves."[20] Self-awareness is central to becoming whole and connected to God and others. If God dwells in our soul, then being connected to God within us will allow us to be connected to God who is also all around us.

Experiencing a certain deficit of our particular "program for happiness" causes us to develop an alternative way of living in relationship. This is where the toxicity develops. In essence we develop a mask or a costume to hide behind to try to gratify our need for power and control, affection and esteem, or security and survival. *Maybe if I create a mask I will feel safe and get the attention and acceptance that I want. Maybe the mask will be more interesting than the real thing. Maybe the mask is more lovable than I am.*

Interestingly, the terms *masks* and *costumes* are also used in the field of psychology. Shirley Jean Schmidt, M.A., L.P.C., creator of Developmental Needs Meeting Strategy (DNMS), helps patients heal from unmet childhood developmental needs using the imagery of a costume. As the patient heals and grows, the child-state of mind is able to discard the costume as a sign of wholeness and healing—parallel to shedding the false self.[21]

The human condition is so complex that being cut off from the Maker and Lover of our soul affects our psyche, emotions, spirit, body and relationships. Our relationship to God, self and others, including the earth and all its creatures, is distorted. The spiritual journey is about being restored, returning to "the Garden," returning to the love of God. Restoration to wholeness of self and relationship with God and others is offered on "the narrow way." The journey begins by waking up. Following is a quote from my journal just before starting the Camino. These musings depict part of my experience in the initial stages of waking up and in the struggle to leave the comfort of what is known for what is unknown.

> For the past several weeks I've been a bit emotional thinking about leaving my community for this season. These are my people. This is home. In home we find safety, security, familiarity and embrace.
>
> I'm going on pilgrimage to a place not my home, not familiar, not safe. Will I find an embrace?
>
> I'm going on pilgrimage and the way is unknown and the

destination unclear and I think some of the emotion I feel in leaving my community is tied into a deep knowing that I will not be the same when I return.

I'm going on pilgrimage. As I walk, I hope to shed the mold of my false self. Abandoned to all I've known and found security and identity in, I hope to walk more fully into my true self and trust that Christ and the saints that have journeyed before me will accompany me into these places of the unknown. Their presence, assurance and example will breathe into me the courage that I need to fully embrace me and all of God's dreams and intentions for me.

I'm going on pilgrimage. The Camino is not a round trip. There is a commencement and a benediction. I will walk. And as I walk, I will leave behind. I will journey ahead. And I will arrive at an unknown destination.

And then I will start a new journey. I will not turn back. We will not turn back.[22]

Embarking on pilgrimage mirrors the initiation of awakening. In taking the initial steps to wake up, I began to listen to the voices in my head and the pain in my heart that I had long avoided. As my eyes opened, my false self started to come into focus. As I dared to wake from my slumber, chains of female inferiority and subordination revealed themselves. No longer seeking sedation or escape, I gave ear to the lies in my head that said, *Phileena, you are what others need you to be. You are only as good as you are able to meet the needs of others. You exist for the sole purpose of supporting others and helping others realize their dreams. Those dreams that your mother sang of in the morning hours are not yours to be had. You have no dreams to be realized. You don't need dreams. Your purpose as a godly woman is to elevate others to realize their dreams.*

The lies in my head were the voices of my false self that had secretly dominated much of my life. With deepening awareness the journey progressed.

Pilgrimage certainly isn't a round trip and neither is the spiritual journey. It is a progression from one place to another. We don't arrive at a new place in our spiritual life only to regress to the place from which we disembarked. It's funny though—on the Camino we did encounter a few people who were walking in the opposite direction. They had reached Santiago and were walking back. Practically speaking, after arriving at Santiago there is the inevitability of returning home. For some, especially before the time of mass transit, I guess they would more than likely return home the way they came— the pilgrimage route. But the imagery of seeing one walking in the reverse direction struck me as odd. We have but one life to live and we can't do it over. We live life and we reflect and we grieve and we learn from our experiences, but God forbid that we revert or regress or stay in the place from which we have been delivered. The invitation is to make a passage and, once that passage is made, we are prepared for the next part of our life's journey. Pilgrimage is not a round trip. There is a beginning point and end point. And then we embark on a new journey. We don't relive the old one.

As I mentioned before, the Spanish word *el camino* means "the way." Pilgrimage has become for me a *way* to live. As I walked the Camino I often thought of the words of Christ, "I am the way, the truth and the life" (John 14:6). And, "for the way is broad that leads to destruction, and there are many who enter through it . . . and the way is narrow that leads to life, and there are few who find it" (Matthew 7:13-14).

The narrow way speaks to the way of the spiritual journey. To find authentic life, one has to have the will to wake up and embark on the journey. In so doing one submits to the redemptive, though painful, road of transformation. If this is not acceptable, choose the broad way. It may be comforting and fun—like a jaunt through La Rioja (the heart of Spain's wine country), which I have also thoroughly enjoyed—full of vineyards and bodegas (wineries) to delight the senses. But it can also serve as a numbing agent to keep one asleep to the gift of one's life. The difference is in the posture. Both the Camino and a visit to La Rioja can have transformative or destructive purpose. It's all in how one orients and submits his or her life.

The gospel says, "Jesus is *the way.*" The Camino, the posture of pilgrimage, had a way of carving that reality, *the* Reality—Jesus—into me. Waking up and embarking on the journey provides the way to tap into the tangible love of God.

CONTEMPLATIVE PRAYER HELPS ME WAKE UP

Parker Palmer, the respected writer, lecturer, teacher and activist, says that contemplation is any way that our illusions are dismantled and reality is revealed.[23] After a few years of a regular practice of contemplative prayer, my soul was ready for this life-shattering dismantling of illusions.

In the seventies, like a few other Christian monks around the world, a Benedictine from England named John Main rediscovered the ancient Christian tradition of what is known as "pure prayer." Pure prayer was taught widely by the Desert Mothers and Fathers of the third and fourth centuries, but the practice had dissipated some over time.[24] Main experienced the groundedness and growth in faith that this disciplined Christian prayer offers. And so he devoted much of his life to teaching this form of contemplative prayer. Main said that contemplative prayer is

- learning to stand back and allow God to come to the forefront of life

- the step away from self-centeredness to God-centeredness

- leaving the ego behind

- simply being open to Jesus' being[25]

Contemplative prayer disciplines our soul to be attentive to God. I like the way my husband, Chris, explains it. He says contemplative prayer is a prayer of consent that creates "muscle memory." It then becomes easier and more natural to consent to God in active life. In essence, it is pure faith, abandonment to the Creator and Lover of our soul. It is "not a conversation in words but an exchange of hearts."[26]

In the Gospel of John, Jesus says:

If you dwell in me, as I dwell in you, you will bear much fruit; for apart from me you can do nothing. . . . If you remain in me and my words dwell in you, ask what you will, and you shall have it. This is my Father's glory, that you bear fruit in plenty and so be my disciples. As the Father has loved me, so I have loved you. Dwell in my love. If you heed my commands, you will remain in my love, as I have heeded my Father's commands and remain in his love. (John 15:5, 7-10)

This is contemplative prayer: to dwell, abide, be or remain in the love of God. We desperately need to recognize and be rooted in the love of God. According to Keating, this is the first stage of contemplative prayer.[27]

The essence of contemplation is the trusting and loving faith by which God both elevates the human person and purifies the conscious and unconscious obstacles in us that oppose the values of the gospel and the work of the Spirit.[28]

Contemplation is the development of one's relationship with Christ to the point of communing beyond words, thoughts, feelings and the multiplication of particular acts; it is a process moving from the simplified activity of waiting on God to the ever-increasing predominance of the gifts of the Spirit in one's life.[29] In the broadest sense, I understand contemplation to mean creating sacred space to be still, to rest in God, to attend to the inner life, to simply be with God in solitude, silence and stillness.

St. Augustine said that we are restless until we rest in God alone. Contemplative prayer teaches us to rest in God, and in so doing the soul settles out of its fears, anxiety and pain.

Contemplative prayer is a "divine therapy" that helps us wake up. As we give ourselves over to trying to satisfy our emotional program(s) for happiness we distance ourselves more and more from our true self and our belovedness. The energy that this takes tends to increase over time; it requires a lot of energy to sustain an illusion. As we fight to stay asleep, we go deeper and deeper into hiding. We need divine therapy to wake us from our slumber.

> To submit to the divine therapy [in contemplation] is something we owe to ourselves and the rest of humanity. If we don't allow the Spirit of God to address the deep levels of our attachments to ourselves and to our "programs for happiness," we will pour into the world the negative elements of our self-centeredness, adding to the conflicts and social disasters that come from overidentifying with the biases and prejudices of our particular culture and upbringing.[30]

Even some of our best deeds can be laced with violence that we are asleep to. Contemplation purifies our actions. Through contemplation we are able to confront the darkness of our personalities and the emotional investments we have made in false "programs for happiness."[31] As a result we open ourselves to the possibilities of experiencing

- interior freedom instead of pursuing power and control
- divine love instead of craving the affection and esteem of others
- presence of God instead of clinging to security and survival

Growing acquainted with the presence of God through the discipline of silence, solitude and stillness makes way for contemplation. But this discipline takes courage. Whoever we think we are, we find out we're not. Contemplative prayer provides a way to wake up from our illusions and to live into the gift of our life—fully awake, fully alive.

TRYING TO UNDERSTAND THE HUMAN CONDITION

The spiritual journey is an invitation to know God and to be known by God, which presupposes that one finds and knows one's self. Awakening allows for the initial stages of distinguishing between the false and true self. In relationship with God, grace reveals false parts of ourselves and invites us to embrace what is real. We have to abandon what is false for continued growth in wholeness and authentic relationship with God and others. As we press into deeper acquaintance and friendship with God, what is false in our preconceived notions of God, the world and our self burns away. Ancient Christian wisdom calls this experience purgation—a process of spiritual cleansing. As I began my journey, through the grace of contemplation I was waking up. The light of Christ was shining in my darkness and I began to let go of false parts of myself with their hidden motivations and distortions. Jesus was inviting me to greater transformation and freedom.

Keating says that because Christ lives in us, we need not go anywhere to find God; we simply need to stop running away and to be attentive to the One who is within us.[32] Surrender to the spiritual journey, aided by the practice of contemplative prayer, is central to personal growth in attentiveness to the presence and love of God.

Like a person waking from a deep sleep, the soul too is invited to wake up. Jesus spoke of this by inviting Nicodemus to be born again (John 3). The invitation is to embrace the world through the eyes of a child, the child-state of innocence that represents Adam and Eve before the Fall. The Christian invitation is to return—return to the essence of who we are and to the purpose for which we were created. There is a state in our human condition that is pure and innocent and that knows she is full of God, in God, aware of herself and of the paradise of God's creation.[33] Christ's invitation is to return to the Garden—the place that symbolizes perfect relationship with God and humanity—to be born anew and to wake up from our state of slumber to enter fullness of life. But when we wake, the light may shine so brightly that all will seem dark. Longing for truth helps us navigate the darkness.

2

LONGING

ON THE THIRD DAY OF PILGRIMAGE Chris and I walked thirteen miles in five hours from Zubri to Pamplona (famous for its annual running of the bulls)—a day that will always be remembered as the "Phileena Shuffle."

As we started out in the morning I didn't know how I would be able to do it. The previous two days we had walked a total of thirty-two miles, down the backside of the Pyrenees. Given that I was unconditioned and carrying a much-too-heavy pack, my neck, back, hips, knees, ankles and feet were completely overused. I didn't want to complain, yet I was in so much pain. After a cocktail of Tylenol and ibuprofen set in, I began to regain some hope that I could make it through the day's journey. Even though Chris's body also ached, he was incredibly patient and encouraged me. He seemed to have more stamina and determination than I at this stage. We tried to find the mystical path in the midst of our physical distractions of pain. By the last couple of hours, I was literally hobbling because of the pain in my calves. I was moving so slowly—

terribly humbling when people ten-plus years older passed me with such ease. In my humiliation, I hobbled into the city of Pamplona where the cheers of the passersby hit me to the core: *"Buen Camino!"*[1] In light of my condition I thought, *Can I really have a good Camino? Will I really make it to Santiago?* "Hope deferred makes for a sick heart" (Proverbs 13:12). I hoped beyond hope that the Camino would get better for me. Starting out, I wondered if I would make it to Pamplona, let alone walk out of Pamplona the following day. Santiago seemed like a far-off dream.

During pilgrimage, as the road stretched on ahead, a longing crept up within me. With each ache in my tired body I longed to reach Santiago. Engulfed in physical pain, I desperately wanted relief and to experience the joy and peace of attaining my destination. I wondered if I would truly make it. *Would I really reach Santiago? Could I persevere?* There were countless moments when I lost faith and doubted that I would get to Santiago by foot. Many pilgrims end up opting for transportation because of injuries. Less than 5 percent who start in France make it all the way to Santiago by foot. But I didn't want to compromise my journey. I wanted to make it step by step. I cried out to God for assistance.

In spite of the pain and suffering, *walking* to Santiago was important for me. So I put one foot in front of the other day after day, moment by moment. With each agonizing step the voice of God was calling me to greater dependence. I longed to make it.

CHILDHOOD LONGINGS

Longings are like growing pains in that their origins can be difficult to trace, and yet they give indication of something deep and profound, something immediately true of us. In that respect, noting our longings and looking more deeply into them can function as a sort of "thin space," in which God pierces our desires and then redeems them with a more devout understanding for how we can live in relationship to God, one another and all of creation.

I can remember as a young child longing for the school year to end and summer to begin—a transition from one stage of life into the next. I remember feeling like the years would drag on before I finally turned sixteen and got my driver's license—such a milestone in a North American teenager's life. I remember the longing that grew within me once I was first cognizant of a call to mission. I was in fifth grade and the teacher asked all the students what they wanted to be when they grew up. Being in a public school and thinking that most of my peers were not Christian, I was embarrassed to say that I wanted to be a missionary. Their responses seemed much more glamorous than mine: Doctor! Lawyer! Astronaut! But clearly in my heart of hearts I knew I was called to mission. From that point on I secretly longed for that dream to be realized.

I grew up in a lower-middle-class family in Indianapolis. My father was the third son of a simple farming couple from central Indiana; my mother was the only child of a struggling widow from Columbus, Ohio. Though the church where my father ministered for sixteen years did not provide adequate salary or benefits for a family of five, my father frugally managed what little we had to provide for our basic needs. Extras were extremely hard to come by, but Dad made sure we always had proper medical and dental care, good shoes, clothing and supplies for the school year, and a decent, modest family automobile.

Mom and us kids were well taken care of on my father's limited salary and personal sacrifices; we always had the basic necessities even if it meant my father would have to go without. The cost of ministry was felt deeply by him and our family, but we knew that counting the cost was a part of the Christian journey. We may not have had the latest material goods, but we were a family rich in character and integrity—due largely to my father's example. I can remember him praying with me each night before I'd go to sleep. And every morning, I'd find him reading the Scriptures and praying before he'd start his day. Though the church didn't provide for his and Mom's retirement, Dad's wisdom and discipline found a way to put back a little each year to plan for their future. Because of my father's thoughtful, frugal lifestyle they will manage to live out their golden years with adequate provision.

As a family in these circumstances, we struggled to dare to dream, let alone to imagine our dreams could be realized. Together with my older and younger brothers, our collective aspirations as a family were to have enough money for food and clothes. It was a rare but delightful Friday night when we could afford carryout pizza—which I remember enjoying occasionally while watching *The Dukes of Hazzard* as a family. (As conservative as my family was, it's a bit surprising to me that we were allowed to watch that show considering Daisy's "immodest" short shorts. This and *Hee-Haw*'s farm beauties were shocking images of female beauty to behold in our family room.) My family had such meager economic means that we rarely ate meat unless my grandfather butchered a cow and could share some with us, or—my friends get grossed out when I tell them this—if we purchased the occasional can of Spam. I have only fond memories of Spam, though I have never bought it myself. My mom could make a mean fried Spam sandwich!

As a kid I longed for scrumptious food like carryout pizza, instead of make-it-yourself "Chef Boyardee" pizza from a grocery store box; and steak was a rarity that I thought was reserved for the rich. This childhood longing has been made sacred in more recent years. Rather than eating meat with every meal, today I gladly choose to go without it most of the time. Most of the commercial meat produced for consumption in the United States comes at the exploitative cost of the poor and the environment. And the treatment of animals in the meat and poultry industry is generally horrific. As I grow in contemplation, I find myself learning to revere all of creation; every bit of food I eat is a sacrificial offering. But my dietary commitment didn't have such lofty origins; the simplicity of my childhood created a longing that made way for a sacramental view of food that finds its origins in the Scriptures.

> But turn to the animals, and let them teach you; the birds of
> the air will tell you the truth. Listen to the plants of the earth,
> and learn from them; let the fish of the sea become your
> teachers. Who among all these does not know that the hand
> of YHWH has done this? In God's hand is the soul of every
> living thing; in God's hand is the breath of all humankind.
> (Job 12:7-10)

Physical longings are not so unlike spiritual ones. Longing is a necessary movement in the progression of the spiritual journey.

LONGINGS OF A YOUNG ADULT

Growing up under these conditions built character but made ambitious pursuits, like crosscultural mission, hard to realize. Most of the members of my parents' families didn't wander far from their birthplace. Life was simple and pragmatic—love God, love your neighbor and pay your taxes. The furthest I traveled while still living at home was to Florida for a family vacation to Disney World and the beach when I was in eighth grade. This was the beginning of my love for the seaside. My father scrupulously saved pennies for years to give this gift to his children. (Thanks so much, Dad!) Unlike many of my peers, I didn't have a college fund and therefore doubted I'd be able to go to college. When I was accepted to Purdue University I didn't know what to do. I was anxious about how we would pay for it. At that point I had decided to pursue a degree in education. I figured if I ever realized the dream of crosscultural mission, a teacher's training would be practical. But then I felt a call to a different university that would require even more faith: Asbury College, which cost almost double the expense of a state university. Named for the founder of American Methodism, Bishop Francis Asbury, Asbury College is a private Christian liberal arts school located in the Mayberry-like town of Wilmore, Kentucky.[2]

The institution was established in 1890 by a Methodist evangelist, the Reverend John Wesley Hughes.

From the moment my mother and I stepped foot on campus we had a strong sense that this would be a good place for me. We left incredibly inspired for me to attend college there. A longing grew within me to arrive as a student in autumn, but we knew it would take a miracle to convince my father, who had doctrinal views strongly opposing Asbury's Methodist roots. My father grew up in a small country Bible church. His faith tradition supports its own colleges from which it recruits its congregational preachers. My mother, father and older brother all attended the same Bible college based in Cincinnati, Ohio. The thought of sending me to a historically Methodist college was, at the least, a stretch and, at the most, out of the question. But to my surprise, Dad was persuaded without even visiting the campus. I am forever grateful for the countless personal sacrifices he and my mother made to help me pay for my college education. And as if that wasn't miracle enough, amazingly, upon graduation I received the one and only E. Stanley Jones Scholarship, which paid almost all of my school debt, because I was committed to giving my life in service among the world's poor. The scholarship, combined with a few generous gifts from friends, enabled me to be debt free once I joined Word Made Flesh—a rare miracle.

At Asbury, I grew in faith and discovered new and wonderful aspects of God's character. It was at Asbury that I experienced a profound encounter with the grace of God's acceptance and received further direction for my initial call to mission.

DISCERNING A CALL

In college, I remember longing to know what my life would look like post graduation. I eagerly sought God's heart for decisions concerning Christian service and seriously contemplated the possibility that fulfilling a call to mission could mean accepting a call to celibacy. I counted the cost of what it would mean to create geographical distance between my family and me. I sorted through my desires to be married and determined to give up everything and everyone to follow Christ. A mentor at the time encouraged me with Jesus' promise in Mark 10:29-30: "Jesus answered, 'The truth is, there is no one who has left home, sisters or brothers, mother or father, children or fields for me and for the sake of the gospel who won't receive a hundred times as much in this present age.'"

Little did I know then how that promise would be fulfilled.

As time went on, I sought out various mission opportunities until one day I met Chris Heuertz and the call was clarified. Chris was the first person to introduce me to God's heart for the poor, and something in his experiences among the poor in the Middle East and South Asia resonated with my heart's longing—especially the stories of the people of India and his time with Mother Teresa. Mother quickly became for me the most compelling woman to emulate. It wasn't long before the call to mission was merging with a call to marriage—the first miracle of God's provision for family. The call in my heart to respond to a world of poverty weaved with the life of a young man who was also responding to the same call. Over time, it seemed evident that the sacrament of marriage with one another would help us fulfill our dream for a more just and compassionate world. God's provision for family has further expanded—I have countless mothers, fathers, sisters (an added bonus since I have no biological sisters), brothers and children all over the world, on nearly every continent (but only one husband!).[3]

My senior year of college, I prepared to leave the nation of my birth for the first time and visit India. I read everything I could get my hands on about this intriguing and mysterious nation that I felt like I had waited my whole life to find. Amy Carmichael's *A Chance to Die* spoke deeply to me, as did Dominique Lapierre's *City of Joy*. Mother Teresa's *Total Surrender* challenged me to the core. As I read, prayed and prepared, the yearning to be in India grew stronger.

Chris and I spent most of our two years of courtship apart—he in India and I in Wilmore finishing my education. This was before e-mail was widely accessible and international telephone rates were very expensive. So we depended on good ol' fashioned snail mail and would occasionally shell out the expense for a fax. I can clearly remember going to Kinko's and asking the staff to dial a twelve digit phone number which would often be answered by a South Indian with an accent rarely heard in Kentucky or Indiana. Our friend's voice would echo throughout the entire store, and we would have to shout through the speaker, "Faxing! Faxing!" in the hopes that they would hang up before the bill ran too high and we could resend. And boy, was postal mail slow! We'd have to wait between ten days and three weeks to get a letter from one another, and sometimes mail would turn up months after the postage date. Today those letters fill five two-inch deep three-ring binders that my Mammaw (maternal grandmother) and I carefully assembled. The notebook paper, aerograms and postcards intermingled with one another bears witness to the longing within us to be together.

HIRAETH: MORE THAN LONGING

Christopher Webb, an Anglican priest, explains longing with the help of the Welsh word *hiraeth* (pronounced "hear-ithe").[4] One of the places the word *hiraeth* is found in the Welsh-translated Scriptures is Psalm 63:1: "YHWH, my God, you are the One I seek. My soul thirsts for you, my body longs *(hiraeth)* for you."

The word *hiraeth* is not easily translatable into English. It means more than longing. It indicates an all-consuming homesickness. It cuts to the bones, soul and DNA of our being. It indicates a longing for where one belongs.

In John 14:3 we read that Jesus will take us to where he is now. This promise was not spoken to the dead but to the living. And John 1:18 tells us where Jesus is. Jesus is close to God's heart. Jesus lived and suffered his passion so that we might be where he is—close to the heart of Abba God. We don't need to physically die to be there, but we do need to long for this destination. Through longing, thin spaces that separate us from God are penetrated; we are broken and our desire for God grows. The movement of longing makes us vulnerable to and penetrable by the action of God.

What consumes you? What have you longed for with the intensity of homesickness? Longing signifies a desire for more. It stands in stark contrast to the complacent life. Complacency is a stalemate to the journey. Longing propels us forward. It's difficult to sit in the ache of longing, so sometimes we avoid it. But when we embrace that gut-level discontent, we are moving and growing. Because the ache of longing can be so agonizing, it is a consolation to be accompanied by others in the journey.

PILGRIM MIRACLES: GOD'S PROVIDENCE

Discerning one's vocation or purpose in life is not an easy undertaking. In my case, in college, discerning the path for my life coalesced between my faith, my compassion for suffering humanity, my desire to serve in the Majority World and my love for Chris. But these kinds of human desires don't always come together. Often, one has to choose—getting something usually means giving something up. In my case, I chose to give up a traditional life with family. The direction my life was headed meant a certain kind of separation from my parents and brothers. It meant not living in the same town with them and seeing them only once or twice a year. It has been a painful loss that we all grieve, but we do the best we can to support one another in our diverging journeys.

The beautiful thing about being true to the inner Voice directing our path is the provision miraculously given along the way. When we set out to live our life with purpose, the journey can get lonely and difficult. We often face hardships and doubts that threaten to take us off course. It is only the veracity of the inner

Voice and God's provision along the way that sustain us in the midst of the harshest trials.

On the Camino, during trials and obstacles that threatened our journey, Chris and I were blessed to experience God's providence through what are known in Spain as "pilgrim miracles." We had heard about such mysteries through various literature we'd read about the Camino, and we came to know personally their reality.

On a day when I wondered if my knees would finally give out, I was desperate for a walking stick. Other pilgrims had told us that walking sticks absorb more than thirty percent of the shock that the knees naturally take in. There was no question from the pain I was experiencing that my knees, as well as my hips and ankles, had been terribly overused.

On this particular day we remembered hearing about an old Spanish man who was known for crafting walking sticks for pilgrims out of hazel wood—the traditional pilgrim staff.[5] Señor Pablito's home happened to be on our route that day. As we ventured into the tiny, quaint village of Azqueta we took a short detour and found two staffs waiting for us outside the elderly farmer's cottage. We couldn't find Señor Pablito, but there were exactly two staffs waiting for us—and just our size![6] It was like he knew we were coming and made provision for us before we could even ask.

Other pilgrim miracles marked our days. One of our friends prayed before we left the States that we would have a bed every day, and even in the most crowded villages we did indeed have a bed each night. This is no understated miracle. In 2003 more than 65,000 people made pilgrimage to Santiago, and accommodations are in short supply during the busy season. Convents, monasteries, guest houses and hotels provide what is available, but some villages are quite small with few beds to offer. It's not uncommon for weary pilgrims to show up in a town after walking twelve to twenty-five miles to discover that all the beds have been taken. The pilgrim is then left to either walk another ten to fifteen miles to the next village or stay in the open air. At one point, after a twenty-four-mile walk to Santo Domingo, we were tempted to panic because all of the pilgrim houses and hotels were full. But the town took pity on all of the exhausted pilgrims and decided to open up the public gymnasium. We slept comfortably that night on old gymnastics mats.

Further miracles occurred through the lives of fellow pilgrims. In the middle of our journey, when we were feeling lonely for companions, three angels found their way into our lives and hearts: Simone, an Italian nuclear physicist from Paris; Miriam, an Italian pharmacist; and Markus, an East German cardiologist. Their joy, enthusiasm and aid in a number of ways lightened our load and encouraged our spirits. We journeyed together—Simone carried some of the contents of my pack; Markus nursed all of our blisters, even performing very minor surgery in some cases; and Miriam comforted us with her warm embrace and joyful demeanor. Though these miracles supported us in the journey, they couldn't dismiss the longing to reach Santiago that etched deeper into my heart, soul and weary body with each pain-filled step.

During seasons of longing, sometimes miracles occur—walking sticks are found, beds are provided, new friends are made, college education is supplied, the call is clarified, a spouse is met and family is multiplied in unusual ways. Following our dreams is not easy. The longing intensifies the longer we persevere in the journey, and all kinds of obstacles threaten to deviate us off course. God's provision along the way reassures us that we're on the right path and encourages us to keep going.

People like Mahatma Gandhi, Oscar Romero, Martin Luther King Jr. and Dorothy Day bore witness to longing. With their entire being they yearned for that which was yet to be realized. By faith they endured and hoped for the promises of a world that reflects the reign of Christ—peace, justice, equality. By their longing they experienced brokenness—they faced head-on some of the most humbling aspects of their human condition, and they were confronted with their limitations as well as their power. Gandhi, Romero and King were even martyred for daring to yearn for something more.

My community emulates this longing. Together we yearn with our lives for a better world, a world where diversity is celebrated and equality realized—male and female, black and white, rich and poor coming together in a full expression of the God who created us. We long for both the victim and the oppressor to be set free. My friend Taylor, a member of the Omaha nation, echoes this perspective. His grandmother would tell him, "We try to extend our hand to our enemy and the enemy of our most vulnerable friends and remind them that they and we are human—we both have a mother and a father and we belong to one another whether we like it or not."

The international offices for Word Made Flesh are based in Omaha, Nebraska. The name *Omaha* comes from the Native American tribe of the same name and translates as "going against the current." I can't think of a better location for Word Made Flesh to call home. The Omaha tribe is known for its countercultural perspective on tribalism: the Omaha people emphasize common humanity, seeing their enemies and the enemies of the vulnerable in their midst as belonging to one another as members of a common family.

The Word Made Flesh community demonstrates our collective longing for the global family through activism expressed in building communities of justice and compassion. Like pilgrimage, there are times when we feel we can't go on. We grow weary, we are injured along the way, our hope wavers. At times we are desperate for miracles of providence to keep us going. We long for *compañeros*[7] to join us—they are essential in the journey of creating a just world. In, with and through community the dream for a better world is realized.

But the dream takes time. All at once we *long for* and *move toward* the realization of our dreams. At times, it may feel like we're getting nowhere, but the longing is moving us. In this way, we participate in a sacramental lingering or vigil.

Seasons of longing in my life have been some of the most intense experiences. In the yearning, space is made in me for the work of God. I am forced to wait and surrender. And there's a sense of restlessness that foreshadows the rest that is coming. When God is doing a new thing, the restlessness stirs up out of an ache for change, birth and new life. Rest comes when what is longed for is realized.

KEEPING VIGIL

Longing. Waiting. This is a movement of the soul in which one can do nothing but linger.

Do you ever waken in the middle of the night unable to go back to sleep? Do you toss and turn and fight with all your might to will yourself to sleep, to no avail? These nighttime disturbances can be an invitation to vigil. Cistercian monks like the ones at the St. Benedict's Monastery in Snowmass, Colorado, rise purposefully in the middle of the night for vigils. During the deep silence of the moments between midnight and dawn, prayer is an act of keeping vigil, waiting before the Lord. Waiting in this manner bids listening.

Longing is about waiting. Longing *is* waiting. Any mother who has labored and delivered a baby knows what I'm talking about. I don't have children of my own, but on January 2, 2009, I had the privilege of waiting through the night while my sister-in-law labored with her second daughter. We got the call around midnight. Chris's brother Adam and his wife, Winter, were headed to the hospital. Winter's labor had begun, resonating profoundly with the winter of my soul and my own longing to bring forth new life. Chris and I were so excited for them we couldn't sleep. So Chris called Adam to check on them after they were settled and they invited us to come over.

It was the middle of the night, so the maternity ward was pretty quiet save a few crying newborns. At first, Winter was fairly comfortable—tired but comfortable. We talked and walked together periodically. As time went on, the contractions got closer and more intense. As Chris and I struggled to stay awake, Winter moaned and groaned in between restless slumber, reminding me of my own struggle to stay alert to the painful reality I had awakened to in my soul. We waited . . . and waited . . . and waited. In the dark labor and delivery room there was very little we could do. We just entered into moments of waiting for the birth of Claire Jula. The hours stretched into the early morning. Labor progressed and before I knew it, the doctor was coming in to deliver the baby. All the months of preparing for this little one, all the sacrifice that Winter made with her body to develop another, all the long hours of labor were finally bringing forth new life. Winter's birth canal was widening and untold miracles were taking place in her body to prepare the way for the baby.

The season of longing in our lives is a crucial time for listening. We listen to the desires within us and to the voice of God in those desires. We wait and listen and learn the will of God. As we wait, we become more acquainted with the presence of God. As we wait, we submit ourselves to the action of God and thus bring forth new life.

Macrina Wiederkehr, in her book *Seven Sacred Pauses: Living Mindfully Through the Hours of the Day,* reminds us that the quality of our waiting can vary. She writes, "There is a difference between waiting and keeping vigil. Anxious, fretful, impatient waiting is nothing more than waiting. Waiting with purpose, patience, hope and love is *vigilant* waiting."[8]

One of the most common images of vigilant waiting is the caterpillar in her cocoon. Butterflies are celebrated as something fascinating and beautiful, but the process of becoming a butterfly doesn't happen overnight. No matter how much the caterpillar yearns to become a butterfly, she must wait. And the process of metamorphosis is anything but gentle. Rid your mind of light and airy, carefree "Flight of the Bumblebee" thoughts.[9] Vigilant waiting can be one of the most distressing experiences in our soul's journey. Change is agonizing. Waiting can be turmoil.

Thanks to nanoscience we know a bit more about what the caterpillar goes through during the long waiting of metamorphosis. In a lab at UCLA, scientists use high-tech tactile microscopes to read the vibrations inside the chrysalis. Those vibrations are then transformed to audio. At the suggestion of my friend, I listened to those sound waves through a report on *Studio 360*.[10] The sounds are like that of an agonizing cry.

Long waiting is not sheer passivity. The English words "passive" and "passion" are both derived from the Latin word *pati*, which means "to endure." Waiting evokes both passivity and passion. Sue Monk Kidd, in her book *When the Heart Waits: Spiritual Direction for Life's Sacred Questions,* writes,

> [Waiting is] a vibrant, contemplative work. It means descending into self, into God, into the deeper labyrinths of prayer. It involves listening to disinherited voices within, facing the wounded holes in the soul, the denied and undiscovered, the places one lives falsely. It means struggling with the vision of who we really are in God and molding the courage to live that vision.[11]

Longing is essential to brokenness. Brokenness is the realization that our false self is dominating, which causes us to be alienated and isolated from God and one another. Through brokenness we recognize our wounded condition and admit that we cannot heal ourselves. Transformation is possible when we accept our brokenness and long for that which only God can do for us. A circular and interdependent relationship develops between longing and brokenness.

THE LONGING CONTINUES

One night during this intense season of longing for changes in me to be realized—for my true self to be freer to emerge—Chris and I had a spirited exchange. The old Phileena was happy to hide in the background, gladly pushing her husband forward and denying herself at every turn like a good, "submissive" woman. Though Chris completely supported and in a lot of ways called forth the more assertive Phileena, we struggled to know how to make appropriate room for two equal but different self-assertive individuals sharing one marriage. The changes in me toward female self-assertion were bumping up against both of us in new ways. We were colliding with one another. Old patterns for how we related to one another were being challenged and the new creation of our transforming marriage wanted to overthrow the old rule. Chris and I couldn't help but to have been shaped by the patriarchal society and religious culture in which we grew up.

Ancient paradigms rooted in male superiority still pervade the minds and teachings of people today. Throughout history, societies have propagated the notion that people could be owned, including wives. In fact, women have been seen as similar to animals—which is even noted in the Hebrew Scriptures. Frequently, women were listed alongside livestock and servants (Exodus 20:17; cf. Deuteronomy 5:21; Judges 5:30). It's interesting that in a lot of cases animals are treated better than some women—dogs affectionately get the favored title of "man's best friend," while women have often been referred to as the "ball and chain" or demeaned by associations such as "You run like a girl"—enforcing the view that women are untrustworthy and the inferior and weaker sex.

These disempowering notions are steeped into cultures the world over. Particularly, these attitudes permeated ancient Mediterranean cultures, religions and philosophies that have had such pervasive influence on present-day Western culture—most notably Christianity. Some of the more prominent Christian Fathers demonstrate the influence of patriarchy in their teaching. The faith tradition we call "Christianity" has never existed apart from these influences. These teachings have dominated religion and culture for so many hundreds of years that it can be difficult to determine where the gospel of Christ ends and misogyny begins.

Augustine, a father of Christendom, is highly debated by theologians as one who perpetuated patriarchy. But his writings also illustrate his countercultural perspective. The truth is that early Christians were unable to completely escape the dominant conscience of the time that viewed women as inferior and subordinate to men. Even though Augustine affirmed the ontological equality of women, it can be argued that he perpetuated some tenets of sexism that we are still trying to identify, confess and repent of today. Though a devout follower of Christ, even Augustine was influenced by the patriarchal mindset of his day.[12]

And so the ideology of female inferiority still infects many aspects of religion, culture and society. Though we've come a long way in redeeming the oppressive perspective of women, the prejudices run deep. Women and men both are guilty of adhering to and perpetuating a demeaning view of women. And Chris and I had to come to terms with the ways in which we had both been influenced by this repressive ideology.

In contrast to power paradigms that repress women and rob men of their holy potential, liberation is central to the message of Christ. It seems that personal and systemic liberation is the common, prominent cry of humanity. Whether it is longing to be free to live into our true self or yearning to be freed from systematic oppression like inequality or slavery, the gospel of Christ is about freedom. But for some reason freedom frightens us, and so two thousand years later we are still subjugating ourselves or expecting others to submit to a posture or system of captivity rather than liberation.

In order for our marriage to endure, the changes occurring in me required changes in Chris. Submission as mutuality would require us to learn a new dance, with its own music and rhythm. We needed to learn new ways of receiving from one another. The two of us were being transformed by awakening. Each of us, and our marriage, was experiencing a metamorphosis. In our longing to be free, we cried out at one another in agony. We desperately tried to communicate our different experiences and perspective. We were in turmoil, much like the caterpillar in its cocoon. But we didn't need a high-tech microphone to hear our distress and anguish—the torment was obvious. We wanted to break free from our suffocating cocoons. We longed for the metamorphosis to be over.

The only sure thing we knew was what and who we were before. We didn't know what lay ahead. It seemed easier to me to submit to a traditional patriarchal paradigm of marriage that was ground into me from an early age and reinforced in so many spheres of my life. If I would just accept my "repressive place" as a woman, Chris and I wouldn't fight with one another and we would experience the feeling of closeness—even if it was an illusion. Marriage marked by male-dominant superiority and female-subordinate inferiority has a long cultural and religious history. It is presumed right and fail-safe. But what if our constructs of safety keep us asleep to God's desires?

PERSEVERING IN THE JOURNEY

The temptation at this stage is to abandon the spiritual journey and opt for what is safe and secure and previously known. We are faced with a choice: push through the pain or give up. The story of the Hebrew people illustrates this human tendency. Even though they yearned for the land God promised, they were tempted to go back to Egypt where they originated—the land of their bondage.

During their exodus from Egypt, the Hebrews demonstrated longing. When God rescued them from their slavery, God brought them into a journey to the Promised Land—a long journey lasting forty years. We know from the Hebrew Scriptures that Moses, the leader of this forty-year wilderness-wandering people, most certainly longed for the land God had promised them. The Hebrews ultimately longed not for where they came from but for where they were heading. They ached for something different and better. But during the long wait, there were periods of time in which some of the people actually wanted to go back to Egypt. The journey was long, the way unknown and difficult. And they had no guarantee that they would end up in a better place. All they had was their faith and the trust that God would indeed meet their heart's longing for the Promised Land.

In the spiritual journey we also face moments of temptation to return to the land of our slavery. It's safe, secure and known. Where God is taking us is risky and unknown and requires deeper trust, courage and greater maturity. No matter the nature of our awakening—feminine or masculine—each of us faces aspects of our human condition from which we long to be free. Perhaps the bondage is an addiction or a self-perception, an attitude or a posture. Whatever the shade of our personal slavery, longing forces us to actively wait, thereby keeping us anchored in the journey toward freedom. We long for what we hope for and are certain of what we do not see.[13] This kind of longing keeps us submitted to the transformational work of God in us.

Chris and I continued trying to find our footing together. Longing for transformation in one another and in our marriage anchored us in the journey. In his exhausted anguish that one heated night, Chris said that all of this was new for us, that we didn't know our way, but that we would find our way together. The morning brought renewed promise of transformation as we held one another and tried to not laugh at the absurdity of our behavior the night before.

The invitation in the season of longing is the prayer of faith. The prayer of faith is different from praying *with* faith. In the first, faith is the mode of prayer. In the latter faith is the object of prayer. The prayer of faith necessitates an experiential relationship with God in which I let go of control and let God be God. I let God introduce God's self to me in an existential way. I come to God in prayer based on pure faith in God's existence within me and beyond me. Preconceived notions of who I think God is are abandoned for the purer, truer Reality that *is* God, revealed by God in God's essence. Prayer of faith is based in relationship with God rather than in what other people say about God. In this posture we believe that God can do for us what we cannot do for ourselves. For months, this in fact was the only prayer I could pray: "God, please do for me what I cannot do for myself." And then all I could do was wait; and the longing within me carved deeper and deeper into my soul, making space for the work of God.

I longed for greater freedom, for new life, and I waited. Like a grain of wheat, death would be inevitable to bearing fruit. Darkness was slowly creeping in.

3   DARKNESS

A woman's body, like the earth, has seasons

When the mountain stream flows, when the holy thaws

When I am most fragile and in need,

It was then, it seems God came closest. . . .

And God is always there, if you feel wounded.

[God] kneels over this earth like a divine medic,

And [God's] love thaws the holy in us.

TERESA OF ÁVILA, "WHEN THE HOLY THAWS"

OUR FIRST DAY ON THE CAMINO involved hiking the verdant and breathtakingly beautiful Pyrenees. Having never really even day-hiked before (unless you count hoofing it all day through the streets of some of the poorest urban centers in the world), Chris and I had no idea what we were getting into. Our mountain-loving friends Andy and Andrea tried to prepare us, but we ignorantly overlooked some of their recommendations. We were far from what we would later understand as "conditioned." Many people train months in advance, breaking in their boots and bodies by taking long hikes with heavy packs on their backs. Chris and I, however, hadn't trained at all.

In the early morning we rose before daybreak, laced our boots and slung our packs on our backs with eager anticipation. It wasn't long before we found ourselves climbing and descending the lush mountains. We walked through various terrain and even more varied weather—blazing sun followed by dropping temperatures that fluctuated fifty degrees. Our bodies moved us up rocky pathways as we ascended above the tree line and down precipitous descents. Upon reaching the summit, after about five hours of this excruciating physical feat, we found ourselves in hypothermic conditions and ended up in a hailstorm.[1]

During the storm on the peak, when the temperature drastically dropped, I hit my first "wall"— the physical, mental and emotional limit that climbers and athletes describe. Remarkably, the human spirit can break through these walls time and time again. This was my first real mountain-hike experience; my pack was much too heavy and my body was out of shape. Enduring the change in temperature from damp cold to a burning warm sun before the weather plummeted to subzero temperatures was a lot for my body to handle all in one day; I was overextended. My neck, shoulders, back, hips, legs, feet and muscles I didn't know I had ached in a way I'd never known before. Mentally and physically I didn't know how I could continue. I had never hit this big of a wall before.

My body, mind and emotions all reached their limit at virtually the same time. Every muscle, bone, joint and tendon seemed to be shouting for me to stop. To make matters worse, my internal feminine cycle would *not* be stopped. Though much of my body wanted to lock up, yes, on the summit of the Pyrenees—day one of our pilgrimage—my body cried out "woman" in crimson red! My abdomen started cramping and my mind felt foggy. Fatigue was setting in throughout my entire body. The ushering forth of womanly lifeblood caused a drain on my physical stamina. How I wanted to curl up in a fetal position and rest! Though it was counterintuitive to impede our journey, in order to take care of feminine necessities, I momentarily had to.

As soon as Chris and I stopped, we realized how much the temperature had plummeted. Our extremities began to tingle from the cold and our sweaty backs suffered a sharp chill. A Buddhist who had stopped with us anxiously pulled out his gloves and wool cap (we, of course, didn't think to pack those!) and warned us of the dangers of frostbite. He told us to not stop for more than a few minutes. The danger in these conditions was worsened by the fact that our bodies were so warm and sweaty from the ascent; we might not know the effects of the cold before it was too late.

Frantically, I found as private a place as I could behind some rocks and brush and dug through my pack for the Tylenol and other provisions. In the process of attending to the womanly essentials, my bare backside got a stark freeze that alerted me pretty quickly to the dangerously icy temperature.

Once my emergency was hurriedly brought under control, it was time to continue. It felt near to impossible to sling that heavy pack back on my back. Everything in me wanted to find a warm place to rest, but there was no shelter from the elements. We had to keep moving. I couldn't stay there. I had run into a wall and didn't know how I would climb over it or get through it. I felt depleted and defeated, and I'd just begun. But like endurance athletes know, amazingly I was able to keep going. Somehow I managed to put one foot in front of the other and carry on. I overcame the first wall.

As time went on and we had still not reached our destination, emotional breakdown number two hit—another wall. I had already extended and overcome my physical limits once, and my body wanted to rest. The hailstorm had intensified its rage with rain and snow, and the temperature continued to fall. I cried a soft cry of agony and told Chris that I didn't know how I could continue, but there was nowhere to stop and rest and take shelter from the elements. Chris encouraged me and helped me recover perspective, and remarkably I made it through the second wall. If I had stopped we would have surely died of hypothermia.

After this grueling experience of extending my limits for the second time, we finally began to descend. The end was in sight—at least mentally if not physically. The rain and snow continued to fall but the temperature started to rise a bit. Unbeknownst to me at the time, we had gotten off the trail. Chris was carefully navigating our way, but in the storm we missed an important marker and took a wrong turn. We were descending, but off the beaten path. Our destination was still not in sight; we had to keep moving.

The rain began falling harder and harder as we wound our way through trees, brush and muddy earth, lost in a lush forest. Despair started setting in because, after all these agonizing hours, we had no idea how far we were from the end. With one more weary, heavy-laden step I slipped in a mudslide and landed flat on my back. That was it! Emotional breakdown number three with a vengeance! The third wall I hit was even bigger and more intimidating than the other two. Sitting in a stream of muddy rainwater pouring down the mountainside, I was beyond depletion and defeat. My tears mixed with rain and mud, and I knew I couldn't go on. We had descended, so the threat of hypothermia had lifted, and everything in me wanted to stay flat in the mud and pray for another day. Chris turned around to find me in my muddy mess and compassionately said, "Honey, we can't stop here. You can do it. It won't be long." Again somehow I got to my feet. We walked about two hundred yards more and, through the trees, spotted the monastery that would provide shelter, food and a bed for the night.

Eight hours after setting out, following three emotional breakdowns and thinking each time I'd reached my limit and could go no further, we arrived at the ancient monastery of Roncesvalles on the eastern border of Spain. An old, gothic stone hall that held one hundred pilgrims would be our shelter for the night. We marveled at the feat we endured and what we had accomplished together.

Attempting to shower and find dinner with the few hours of daylight we had left, we realized we could barely walk and wondered how in the world we would rise the next morning and set out again. We ached from head to toe and everywhere in between. Sleep never felt so good—even with the cacophony of snorers from around the world sharing our medieval shelter.

In the early morning of the next day, waking to the sound of Gregorian chant, we discovered how remarkable the body is: as we slept, our bones, muscles and joints rejuvenated themselves enough that we could walk again. During the darkness of night, there was a restorative work taking place in the dark and hidden places of the body—a sign of the genius of God's creation. Like a woman's menstrual cycle, I was experiencing the benefits of the hidden and darker elements of life. In the cyclical fashion of menstruation, the body was remaking itself. My soul was experiencing a similar effect from the darkness it was experiencing. The secret work of God was transforming me.

We could indeed walk again—though not without significant pain, a natural consequence of being out of shape and carrying a much-too-heavy pack. The pain of that first morning would become my companion every day on the Camino. What inspired us as a perceived romantic stroll through Spain quickly became a rude awakening to the ancient act of pilgrimage for purification. Chris and I decided to lighten our packs of everything but the most essential items for the journey—a process we took part in several times along the way. It's embarrassing to list the things I packed that I clearly could have done without: a travel-size hairbrush, retractable clothesline, travel umbrella, fleece, fourth pair of socks, and books. As I simplified, I abandoned myself to my limitations and the rules of the road. Pilgrimage would have to be made with simplicity and a desire to be free.

Each morning we set out, we prayed with all of our hearts that God would give us the grace to make it to Santiago. With each painful step, we found ourselves in the company of pilgrims from past centuries who bathed the way before us with their prayers and tears, injuries and sicknesses, pain and joy. In the company of these *compañeros,* we were indeed accompanied with grace. As E. Allison Peers says, "Grace, far from destroying nature, ennobles and dignifies it."[2]

As the days progressed, the Spanish countryside rolled out before us as a grand display—the greenest green and bluest blue were before us as far as the eye could see. The reddest poppies and whitest daisies sprung up to line our path and tickle our senses. When we entered La Rioja, the vineyards spoke to us of life and fecundity found in being connected to the vine. My thoughts returned often to the words of Jesus: "I am the vine; you are the branches. Those who live in me and I in them will bear abundant fruit, for apart from me you can do nothing" (John 15:5).

In a spirit of mutuality, there were days when I leaned on Chris and days when he leaned on me. One day we passed through what seemed like the Hobbits' quiet, rural village. There was a small forest of the most magnificently shaped trees I had ever seen. I really felt we had been transported to another world. As we passed through this magical countryside, Chris was really struggling. The pack on his back weighed down heavily and was causing him a lot of pain. The stamina and determination of earlier days failed him at this point in the journey. He was struggling to find any inspiration to keep going. It's amazing how when one is weak the other is strong. A depth of courage and determination rose within me and I encouraged him to keep going. Every time his eyes would drift down to his feet I would remind him to look to the horizon and to let it pull him forward. I would periodically call out to him, as he had to me, "We're doing this Bebe!"

We walked. Every day, we walked. We alternately supported

one another when one was feeling disheartened. Finding the courage and the stamina to return to the Camino each day grew more and more difficult. Our necks and backs ached constantly. The joints in our hips, knees and ankles seemed to rub together and often there would be kinks in them—their overuse was apparent. The chronic pain was like nothing I'd ever known before. I clung to the hope that "though this physical self of ours may be falling into decay, the inner self is renewed day by day" (2 Corinthians 4:16).

DOUBT AND ABANDONMENT: THE BEGINNING OF DARKNESS

When I set out on the Camino, I hadn't fully realized what I was getting into. Darkness came in waves. I couldn't avoid or go around the dark physical and mental feats I faced. I had to pace myself with it and go through it. We can't skip over or outrun darkness; neither can we hide from it in the busyness of life or in a time of extended rest, such as my time at Duke.

After the Camino, as I transitioned from a very active life of service into a long, deep, contemplative rest in Durham, I experienced a necessary yet difficult detachment. Like the experience of the feminine cycle, I was transitioning from one phase and God's activity in it to another. Progressing from one stage to the next is not easy—it is filled with discomfort, pain and disorientation. But it is ultimately life-giving, actually essential to the creation of life.

I was quite familiar with the active, engaging, busy stage of life—the Phileena who jetted across the globe in partnership with her husband to build communities of justice. But I was not at all prepared to explore the deeper, more complex phase that was waiting for me.

On the Pyrenees, as I faced the unknown and experienced feats completely new to me, doubt crept in. *Am I really capable of climbing this mountain—let alone, walking all the way to Santiago?* Similar questions haunted me during the Duke portion of sabbatical as I detached from my life of activism—an experience completely new to me. *If I'm not actively supporting and serving the movement of Word Made Flesh, who am I?* I questioned my identity, abilities and gifts. I was making a gradual descent of the soul.

My experience at the peak of the Pyrenees is a powerful symbol of the spirituality of descent. It's only when we can experience and embrace our deepest pain and suffering that we can emerge transformed. Richard Rohr, a Franciscan monk and founder of The Center for Action and Contemplation located in Albuquerque, New Mexico, wisely highlights the inherent rites of passage unique to the woman. Within her very biology she is given the symbol of blood and the experience of vulnerability from which to draw true courage. At menstruation, childbirth and menopause, the woman is initiated into a passage—from old to new, death to life, weakness to strength. Blood for her is a sign of life. In contrast, a man's blood often triggers for him feelings of death. Perhaps because of the void of this inherent biology, traditionally and historically men have instituted rites of initiation; the symbol of blood and embrace of one's weakness is typically a universal common denominator in these rites. In our modern society, perhaps the lack of such intentional formation creates new challenges for male spirituality.[3]

As the weeks of rest unfolded at Duke, I succumbed to a spiritual descent. I felt like I was in a dark tunnel. I was struggling to find my way. Everything grew dim—my sense of self and my understanding of God. I knew the God who was actively engaged in a world of poverty. I had encountered Christ in the dying, naked man at Howrah Train Station in Kolkata;[4] the child soldier in Sierra Leone; the young mother on the streets of Lima. But who is this God who allows me to rest from a world in need and to engage the beauties of Spain? These questions gave rise to doubt. *Do I really know God at all?*—this God who seems to be suggesting through sabbatical rest that God is interested in me as well as in those I serve. I began to question my identity and what I knew of God.

And doubt gave rise to internal pain that I was not aware of before. I felt like I was in a stone mortar being ground by a pestle. Like the physical pain on the Camino, emotional pain became a constant torturous companion. And because of its presence, I felt abandoned by God. I was left with more questions and seemingly no answers. Anything I had found false security in (the "known")— like my identity in relationship to people and my acts of service— was being challenged and I knew not what the other options would be (the "unknown"). *If I am not what I do, not defined by my relationships with others, who would I be if or when I emerged from this grinding? Would I be anything more than dust?*

For months prior to this dark night experience I prayed daily the prayer of St. Ignatius:

> Take O Lord and receive
> All my liberty, my memory,
> My understanding and my entire will
> All that I have and possess
> You have given all to me
> To you O Lord I return it
> All is yours
> Dispose of it all according to your will
> Give me your love and grace
> For this is sufficient for me.

St. Ignatius of Loyola (1491-1556) was the founder and first superior general of the Society of Jesus, also known as the Jesuits. He is marked as one who gave everything to Jesus and who lived a devoted life of prayer and activism. He influenced the movement that became known as the Catholic Reformation[5] and remains an example for how to integrate the contemplative and active dimensions of the gospel.

When we earnestly pray the prayers of saints, I believe we are invited into a treasured storehouse. Praying the prayers of those whose lives are explicitly marked with the life of Christ has transformational power. The saints lived the prayers they prayed. Their prayers made way for a deep inner work of Christ in their lives. When we pray in a posture and attitude related to that of the saint who wrote the prayer, a similar transformation is made possible for us.

Rather than *me praying*, after some time it seemed as if the prayer of St. Ignatius was *being prayed* in me. I found myself asking, *Did I really pray for the "taking"?!* The "taking" was painful and frightening for I knew not what awaited me. Even if what was being taken was ultimately bad for me, it was all I'd ever known. It was familiar. It felt better than the nothingness with which I was seemingly left.

My prayer was being answered, but I couldn't have imagined the experience of how it would be answered. God was taking my liberty in the spirit of the prayer of Ignatius. Even my prayers were no longer my own. Everything was being taken from me at my bidding—my freedom, memory, understanding and entire motivation for life, relationships and service. I was abandoned to the cry of this prayer. And thus I began to be stripped of some of the false parts of myself that were expressed in false identities and false attachments, the parts of me that kept me from faith, hope, love and peace—in essence, from God. Trusting by faith that God truly knows what is best for me, I invited God to take everything from me that would inhibit my growing nearer to God—the destination of my soul. I was abandoning myself by faith to my Creator.

During the first portion of sabbatical, on the Camino, abandonment was doubt's *compañero*. The material abandonment that was required to make pilgrimage in Spain is not so different from what it takes to make spiritual pilgrimage. I had to leave behind everything but what I thought would be essential for the journey. And then even along the way I had to shed a number of items in my pack

that were weighing me down and threatening to impede my journey and keep me from reaching Santiago. In the first few days of
the Camino I unloaded my pack of what at one time seemed essential, but in reality was cumbersome and even damaging to my
body because of the added weight. I was growing in clarity for
what truly would be necessary for pilgrimage. Letting go of certain
possessions opened me to greater freedom in the journey.

This sort of abandonment invites a kind of darkness. The comfort of my possessions on the Camino provided security for me,
like light on a dark road. I had something for every need I could
anticipate: books for boredom, a line to dry wet clothes and a hairbrush for vanity. With possessions in tow, my life was somewhat
predictable and sure. Shedding some of those things invited a detachment and feeling of abandonment from what was sure and secure. Letting go of several possessions was an act of deeper faith
that I would be sustained on the journey beyond what I could do
or provide for myself. Being free of certain material attachments
meant facing the darkness of the unknown.

During the Duke portion of sabbatical, I spent the first several
weeks in deep reflection and prayerful meditation, aided by the ther-
apeutic exercise of gardening. The Rose Cottage—our home away
from home—was an answer to prayer and a gift of God. The front
and back yards provided an entire landscape in which I could get my
hands dirty and reconnect with the earth. As I weeded the overgrown
yard, it was as if an internal uprooting was taking place in me.

For those first few weeks, I could hardly do anything other than
gardening. One of the prevailing themes that emerged during that
time was, "From dust you came and to dust you will return" (Genesis 3:19). If there was no promise of who I was or who I would
become, if no promise of a secure self and a guaranteed personal
contribution after sabbatical, knowing that I came from dust and
would return to dust became surprisingly comforting.

The invitation of the prayer of St. Ignatius is all about abandonment. Willingly, if not fearfully, we can choose to completely leave behind that which we have known and found security in— everything that we have worked hard to attach to by way of creating our identity. "I know who I am and others know who I am based on what I do, what I like, who I'm friends with, what I read, what I have, how I relate to people, my intellectual musings, what others say about me, my kind gestures." Depending on our experience, upbringing and temperament, the attachments will be different.

As we let go of physical, mental and emotional attachments, we abandon ourselves to God and yield without restraint to God's love and grace—for this is sufficient for life's journey. Knowing and being known by God, relationship with God, is supreme—the source of our identity and purpose. Expressing our truest identity is possible when we are free of false attachments that try to make claim on who we are. These accessories can become quite burdensome and impede our pilgrimage. The spiritual journey has to be made with simplicity and a desire to be free.

In darkness, doubt gives rise to important questions. And abandonment allows us to be free from that which threatens to keep us in slumber. But if we've been asleep, we don't know what it will be like to be awake. All seems dark, unknown and somewhat fear-inducing. Fear is actually the most common response in the brain to the unknown. But studies show that when we face our fears and overcome them, our brain develops and grows; and not only our brain, but our body and spirit as well.

Lee Hoinacki in his book *El Camino: Walking to Santiago de Compostela* says,

> The camino is not a path leading to Santiago, but a way to reach Christ—if one can learn how to walk on it. . . . It is an initiatory exercise, teaching one some elementary truths about stripping oneself bare. The further one progresses in

this way, the further one will walk into the mystery of faith, into nothingness, weakness, and darkness.[6]

On pilgrimage I suffered in ways I had never known before. From the first day's mountain climb, my body was ravaged with sore joints and muscles. But by pressing through, I endured a purifying pain in the journey. By overcoming physical, mental and emotional obstacles, I progressed in the journey and received grace upon grace. But the pain I encountered on the Camino was simply a foreshadowing of the inner agony waiting for me. The Camino was indeed an "initiatory exercise." It was preparing me for an inner pilgrimage that would be necessary for transformation. An inner stripping and abandonment was beckoning me.

Following pilgrimage in Spain, when Chris and I relocated to Durham for four months, I stumbled into darkness—a spiritual desolation. I had never felt more spiritually arid, empty and emotionally overwhelmed. I often felt like I was sitting in a muddy mess mingled with tears. I was taken to the depths of my being and identity, but like Chris said in the Pyrenees, Jesus was now saying, "You can't stay here."

IN PRAISE OF FECUNDITY

At the peak of my first mountain climb on pilgrimage—though my body, mind and emotions wanted to give out and give up—a feminine force within me stirred, marked by the onset of menstruation. The red blood symbolizing the capacity to bear fruit from the deepest part of me announced itself as a source of life and energy. The monthly blood flow I experienced at the summit was a symbol of feminine strength within me that longed to be born. This was a birth that required an incubation and gestation period. It would take time. And the delivery of this new life within me would not come without severe trial and anguish—much like a mother giving birth to her child. Darkness was essential for the development of this new life.

Kimberlee Conway Ireton gives some understanding to my experience:

> In Western Christian culture, we tend to oppose light with darkness and assume that since light is good, darkness must be bad. But it is not, necessarily. The darkness of the womb and of the soil, for instance, are places of incubation, gestation and growth. Seasons of darkness in our lives are often good and necessary. . . .
>
> Death is a mystery, veiled and dark. We are tempted to fear this darkness, to forget that the good shepherd is with us, guiding and comforting us. In our fear, we can become hasty, rushing blindly and desperately through the darkness in order to get to the light that must be on the other side. But this we must not do. We must remain in the darkness as long as it takes to learn in death's shadow the lessons we can only learn there. We must wait patiently in the darkness, trusting that God is with us and is growing new life in us. For, Jesus says, only if a grain of wheat falls into the earth and dies will it bear much fruit.[7]

Fecundity. I love this word because it means more than being fruitful. It means having the capacity to bear an abundance of fruit. We like the thought of being fruitful, but we rarely examine what it requires of us to be fruit bearing—discomfort, pain, trial, patience, darkness and labor.

Fecundity speaks to the capacity for fruitfulness. Jesus of course understood this concept and explained it perfectly in pointing his disciples to grapevines. Comparing the connection to the vine with a connection to himself, he revealed the secret to being fruitful. The capacity for fruitfulness is found in relationship to him. That connection provides the capacity to bear real and lasting fruit. And if you appreciate a good glass of wine, you know what it takes to produce such exquisite *vino*. The endurance of the grape is equal to the quality of the wine it can produce. Good wine, like good life, requires arid conditions paired with tender care.

The female womb also symbolizes the ability to bear fruit. Fruitfulness doesn't happen without the capacity for it to happen, and the monthly blood loss and pain presupposes a woman's ability to bear a child. The woman's body and feminine cycle is such important imagery for us and it's a shame that we tend to overlook it. Patriarchal systems that divorce us from the feminine rob us of wisdom and perspective that men and women both need. Male and female are both created in the image of God. When we don't allow ourselves to reflect on the feminine nature of God, our understanding of God is deficient. Similarly, our communities are deficient when they exclude women from central places of influence and authority.

In the Hebrew Scriptures God is referred to as "compassionate." The word for compassion is derived from *racham,* meaning "womb." God is "womblike." In Job God refers to God's self as the One who gave birth to the frost: "Whose womb gives life to ice or gives birth to skies filled with hoarfrost" (Job 38:29). Talk about fecundity! One doesn't have greater capacity to bear fruit than God! The whole created world reflects God's feminine facility for bearing fruit.[8]

Male and female created in the image of God have a certain capacity for fecundity which includes the ability, in most cases, to produce children. But a culture that limits fruitfulness to sexual reproduction misses out on the limitless nature of a God whose intelligent creativity and productivity have no bounds.

Having been created in the image of God, the feminine nature of God reproduced in me was stirring. What it means to be fully me, fully woman, wanted to be born and celebrated—making no apologies for my gender, but instead embracing my nature and offering it as a gift to my community and to the world. But this yearning of life was just a seed. It would require a gestation and incubation period. Darkness was necessary.

STUMBLING THROUGH DARKNESS

At the end of the Camino, I found myself in desolation. During this season of life, darkness encompassed me. Having abandoned along the road all I'd known before of myself and of God, I felt as if I had nothing to give the world and I doubted my faith as never before. In the months following I felt the presence of God rarely, if at all.

St. John of the Cross, a Carmelite reformer and doctor of the church from the sixteenth century, refers to seasons like this as "dark nights of the soul." In his profoundly mystical yet straightforward theological work, he illuminates for his disciples the necessary darkness each must endure to live into the light of their life and relationship with God. Both inviting and terrifying, John of the Cross describes in detail the agonizing yet liberating experience of divine grace in the journey toward divine union. The dark night of the soul is understood in stages, distinguishing between the night of sense and the night of spirit. The first is said to come to many, while the latter comes to few. The first is "bitter and terrible"; the second doesn't compare because it is "horrible and awful to the spirit."[9] St. John's *Dark Night of the Soul* explores in greatest detail the night of spirit because, at the time of his writing, there was little communicated about it, in contrast to the abundance of literature on the night of sense.[10]

Mother Teresa's night of the soul has been highly debated—hers being the longest recorded dark night, lasting most of her fifty years of service among the poorest of the poor. Following the release of her most personal letters and diaries in the book *Come Be My Light,* her intimate dark night experience was subjected to harsh analysis and criticism. Most observers, however, are left to marvel at what she endured. After the release of *Come Be My Light,* Chris and I were routinely asked about Mother Teresa's dark night, since we had the privilege to have met her. Friends wanted to know what we thought about her experience, which is explained in despairing detail in the book. Usually we reply that the time we or members of our community have spent in Kolkata has caused us all to despair and doubt.

Kolkata is one of the most densely populated cities in the world, filled with people suffering from extreme systemic poverty and injustice. Home to approximately sixteen million inhabitants, countless live on the streets or in slums. Spending much time at all among impoverished men, women and children in Kolkata necessitates a very honest questioning and wrestling with God and faith. I don't know of anyone who has matched Mother's downward mobility and incarnational ministry except Jesus. Mother had an exceptionally difficult calling to establish a global effort to honor the poor and disenfranchised, and in doing so she pointed millions to Christ. She forged a path, a movement, a presence in the world that can be compared to none. Her long dark night deserves our respect, not our criticism.

Mother's experience can be understood in spiritual as well as psychological terms. Her experience is complex and all-pervasive. And her experience is hers. Amazingly, through the physical, emotional and spiritual desolation, she kept her faith. The transformation and liberation she experienced because of the darkness we are not privy to. But her life and dark night bear witness to the struggle of the human spirit. Her fidelity to Christ serves as a beacon of light for the rest of us when we courageously face our own darkness.

St. John of the Cross offers this exhortation for those who experience the dark night:

> Realizing the weakness of the state wherein they are, they may take courage, and may desire that God will bring them into this night, wherein the soul is strengthened and confirmed in the virtues, and made ready for the inescapable delights of the love of God.[11]

According to John of the Cross and other saints who have gone

before us, dark nights of the soul are a way by which the Spirit of
God can penetrate our being, purify us and lead us into deeper
faith and more intimate relationship with God. In this way we attain union with the One we were separated from by sin—the dis-
connection expressly illuminated in the Garden story.

Several years prior to being enveloped by this darkness, I had
asked to draw nearer to God. In my naiveté I had no idea that it
would mean an internal descent into darkness. As the weeks unfolded into shadows of death, I realized that "emotional junk of a
lifetime" (as Keating calls it) was situated between me and God. Intimacy is about honesty and trust. To grow in intimacy with God, I
had to face hidden emotional wounds and subsequent "programs for
happiness" and let go of them. As much as God may have wanted to
embrace me, I was not free to be fully known by such an embrace.
And I was not free to know God as God is. Intimacy is not only
about knowing the other but being known as well. I was being invited to come out from hiding and into the agony of God's piercing
light, to eventually emerge into the "inescapable delights of the love
of God." That kind of love could only be experienced through open,
honest intimacy. Darkness was an indispensable agony.

St. John of the Cross likens the darkness of the soul to a log of
wood being burned with fire. In times of darkness, the Light is
actually very near, but our human faculties cannot comprehend
this light, so it seems we are in the dark. A friend of mine explains this experience in a different way: Like a sick child with a
fever, the caregiver nurtures and tends to the little one all throughout the night, but in severe cases of illness the child is not aware
of the caregiver's presence.

Expanding on the image of a burning log of wood, the fire burns
in such a way as to cause us the *sense* of darkness. But in fact, this
fire or light that causes us to feel darkness is really God's grace—a
grace of purgation that heals and makes ready the soul for deeper
union with God. John of the Cross writes,

It is well to observe at this point that this purgative and loving knowledge or Divine light whereof we here speak acts upon the soul which it is purging and preparing for perfect union with it in the same way as fire acts upon a log of wood in order to transform it into itself; for material fire, acting upon wood, first of all begins to dry it, by driving out its moisture and causing it to shed the water which it contains within itself. Then it begins to make it black, dark and unsightly, and even to give forth a bad odour, and, as it dries it little by little, it brings out and drives away all the dark and unsightly accidents which are contrary to the nature of fire. And, finally, it begins to kindle it externally and give it heat, and at the last transforms it into itself and makes it as beautiful as fire.[12]

No other explanation helped me make sense of my experience more than the words of St. John of the Cross. After pilgrimage I spent most of my days at the Rose Cottage at Duke. I would wake each morning and venture into the living room to sit for hours in the big, comfy, floral-print sofa chair. I would sit and try to pray and find myself unable to utter any words. Silence and the flickering of burning wood in the fireplace were my only companions. I would sit in contemplation, with no words to utter. I would sit and desperately search for the presence of God, to no avail. For months I had absolutely no consolation or felt sense of the Presence. I would sit *in* silence, *with* silence; and if I was graced with the ability to gesture toward God at all, it came in the form of tears streaming down my face. The purgation seemed to only intensify as time went on.

Like the wood burning in my fireplace, the "moisture" within me was drying out. Before long there were no more tears to shed. Instead, the dark and unpleasant parts of me began to surface and I could hardly bear to face them. As the fire burned, those unsightly, pain-filled, hurting places in me were being driven out. Though all I could comprehend was desolation, I trusted that I was being healed by darkness and flames. I read *The Dark Night of the Soul* and the complementary book *The Cloud of Unknowing* and took courage.[13] I hoped beyond hope that I was experiencing a *healing* internal fire. The sense of darkness was pervasive, and I longed to sense the light.

As the darkness grew I found myself in a deeper place of fear, doubt and anxiety than I'd ever known.

> Periods of psychological ferment and destabilization are signs that the journey is progressing, not failing. The results can often be horrifying to ourselves. As trust grows in God and practice becomes more stable, we penetrate deeper and deeper down to the bedrock of pain, the origin of our personal false self. In response to each significant descent into the ground of our woundedness, there is a parallel ascent in the form of inner freedom, the experience of the fruits of the spirit and beatitude.[14]

The intense descent to the bedrock of my false self felt destabilizing. It was far from a pleasant experience. I began to face the unknown of my identity and it frightened me. As falsehoods and old affections and attachments were brought to my attention, the invitation was to let them go. Without them I felt as if I had nothing, as if I was nothing. I realized that many of my acts of service were selfishly motivated to fuel a feeling of being loved. If I could meet the needs of others and support them I felt important, needed, wanted, valuable (therefore "loved"). The line between true acts of service or kindness and falsely motivated ones is so thin.

In addition, cultural and religious ideologies that repressed and subjugated "woman" were being stripped away. My very understanding of what it meant to be a woman, what it meant to be "Phileena" was coming undone. Since my previous identity was all

I knew, apart from it I didn't know who I was. A more liberated vision of myself was hard to imagine. Needing the identity that the falsehood offers makes its detection difficult. We can be so easily deceived by ourselves. Courageous surrender and abandonment are the keys to liberation for the true self.

The internal descent, like descending the Pyrenees, was painful and despairing. At times I doubted if I could continue the journey, but St. Paul's exhortation encouraged me: "It is no longer I who live, but Christ who lives in me. The life I live in the body I live by faith in the Son of God who loved me and gave himself for me" (Galatians 2:20 NIV).

Through agonizing darkness, I was learning to abandon myself more fully to Christ's life. Faith was the only thing that kept me anchored. By faith I reached out for Jesus' hand and let him lead me through darkness. Most of the time my only audible prayer in addition to tears was, "Jesus keep me." This state of dependency was humiliating and necessary. Recognizing my need and choosing to depend on God was the beginning of liberation from the sins of pride and self-abnegation. Only in this way could the freedom I longed for be realized. My faith was put to the test like never before during this dark night of my soul.

As months went on, with the aid of a few friends and an incredibly supportive husband, I began to find courage in the paschal mystery of Christ. Jesus' passion, death and resurrection became an invitation to intimacy. Before resurrection comes the torment of the passion that includes unmatched darkness and agonizing death. The great Scottish Christian novelist George MacDonald gives word to my experience:

> To give us the spiritual gift we desire, God may have to begin far back in our spirit, in regions unknown to us, and do much work that we can be aware of only in the results. . . . In the gulf of our unknown being God works behind our conscious-

ness. With [God's] holy influence, with [God's] own presence . . . [God] may be approaching our consciousness from
behind, coming forward through regions of our darkness
into our light, long before we begin to be aware that [God] is
answering our request—has answered it, and is visiting
[God's] child.[15]

Like the hidden work of the body's rejuvenation on the Camino,
God was mysteriously at work in the dark and hidden places of my
soul, remaking me.

A dark night of the soul is not an intellectual exercise but a life-
shattering experience. This kind of experience cannot be crafted
or sought after—it can only be submitted to. Darkness of the soul,
though terrifying, is a profound grace. It is an invitation by the
Spirit to transformation.

4   DEATH

I want to keep my soul fertile for the changes,

so things keep getting born in me, so things keep

dying when it is time for things to die. I want to keep

walking away from the person I was a moment ago,

because a mind was made to figure things out,

not to read the same page recurrently.

DONALD MILLER, *THROUGH PAINTED DESERTS*

DEATH. NO ONE REALLY LIKES TO TALK ABOUT IT. Fewer people embrace it. Death is something we fear and shun. We avoid it at all costs. Our society offers remedy after remedy to help us look young, stay young and prolong life. Death is the last thing most of us want. We avoid it for ourselves and we don't like talking about the death of others.

In contrast, in Kolkata—the city of death—Mother Teresa's Missionaries of Charity have made death a center of attention.[1] They are faithful day in and day out to women and men who are destitute and dying. The ones whom no one can or will look after find a safe and peaceful place to end their lives in Nirmal Hriday,

"Home for the Dying." In this small building attached to the Hindu epicenter of the city, the Kali temple, there are fifty cots for men and fifty cots for women. Men and women from all over West Bengal end up in the Home for the Dying by some of the most extraordinary ways. From the villages surrounding Kolkata, sometimes family members put persons who are desperate for medical attention on the train to the city in hope that they will find the treatment needed. If they have little to no money when they arrive, these ill patients are often forced to beg and are easily manipulated by the underworld of crime that controls the streets. Before long, their health deteriorates even more, and with no one to look after them they begin to waste away, alone. Missionaries of Charity and their volunteers comb the streets and train stations looking for these victims. The lucky ones are found and brought to the Home.

Medical supplies at Nirmal Hriday are in short supply and limited to only the necessities—disinfectant for cleaning wounds, nasal feeding tubes, IV drips for rehydration purposes and a small assortment of pain relievers. Having taken a vow of poverty, the sisters who run the Home use very simple linens and gowns, which are hand washed every day. The most inexpensive tin is their choice of dishware, and this too is hand washed after every meal with a meager blend of soap powder and ash—the soap of the poor.

The patients are invited into these humblest of circumstances that offer a sanitary place to lay their head, the easing of pain and distress through limited resources, and the opportunity to die not alone but in the company of love.

Along the central staircase hangs a large crucifix that reads, "I thirst." Mother Teresa believed that tending to the poorest of the poor—whether materially or spiritually poor—was a way to quench the thirst of Christ in his distress. "Jesus is God," she wrote; "therefore His love, His thirst, is infinite. He the creator of the universe, asked for the love of His creatures. He thirsts for our love. . . . These words: 'I thirst'—do they echo in our souls?"[2]

With similar attention to death, Jon Sobrino writes about "crucified people" persons suffering poverty and oppression.[3] Sobrino, a Jesuit who makes his home in El Salvador, narrowly escaped assassination by the Salvadoran government during the 1989 murder of his six Jesuit brothers, their housekeeper and her daughter. The Jesuits were targeted because of their outspoken stand for justice and peace during the El Salvador civil war that left about 75,000 men, women and children dead (a majority were civilians). People like Sobrino and Mother bring the world's attention to Jesus in the distressing disguise of the poor, and they invite us to connect with him through the lives of the destitute, exploited, imprisoned and dying. Again, Mother's words are penetrating: "Our life of poverty is as necessary as the work itself. Only in heaven will we see how much we owe to the poor for helping us to love God better because of them."[4]

Rather than attempt heroic feats of modern medicine, which is the privilege of the few, wealthy citizens of the earth, Mother—out of her poverty—gave all she had to the least among her. Mother was often criticized by the rich for her method of ministry to these patients. It seems that the wealthy are usually the most uncomfortable with death, while the poor know that death is an inevitable part of life. The few who have access to all kinds of resources often want to impose their will on the world, thinking they are responding with generosity and compassion; yet in some cases their gestures may be more about themselves, their fears and their needs than about selfless consideration for another. Compassion literally means "to suffer with." But few of us are willing to suffer ourselves, let alone to suffer with someone else.

Committed to a vow of poverty among the impoverished, Mother's mission was pure compassion—to suffer with those who suffer while easing their pain as much as possible and in so doing quench the thirst of Christ in his agony on the cross. An obsession with prolonging life was never a part of Mother's paradigm. Mother was not afraid of death. Her life was marked by dying—dying to her desire to stay near to the mother she loved; dying to her culture and choosing the life of a nun; dying to the safe, protected and predictable life of the cloistered convent and choosing to be a poor Indian among poor Indians;[5] and dying to her desire for consolations in her spiritual life.

In the lives of the most vulnerable of the world's poor, Mother encountered Christ. By suffering with her friends in poverty and accompanying them in their distress, she pointed humanity to life that is stronger than death. In Mother's world, death was not to be feared but embraced.

The first time I entered Nirmal Hriday was the summer of 1995—the hottest time of the year, when temperatures frequently skyrocket over one hundred degrees Fahrenheit and you can cut the humidity with a knife. For a few years I had heard heart-wrenching stories about this mysterious place, and then I suddenly found myself on its threshold. I could hear the moans of the people inside and smell the putrid mix of Detol (disinfectant), curry and decaying bodies. Life and death mingled together. I braced myself as I entered, saying a quiet prayer that God would give me the grace to enter such a place. Turning the corner, my eyes immediately made contact with eyes sunken deep in the skulls of the dying. Nuns and volunteers were quietly, meditatively tending to them. Even the stronger patients were caring for the weaker ones. There was a surprising sense of peace in a room filled with death. Grace filled the room's volume like water. It was dense. Grace was given to me by entering. I didn't need grace to enter; I received it by entering.

One afternoon, as I tried desperately to make myself useful—feeding patients, bathing them, singing to them—one woman gestured for me to sit on her cot and, to my astonishment, she insisted on massaging my arms. Death was creeping at her door, yet she embraced me and tended to me—the one who seemed healthier and full of life being ministered to by the dying. Such a paradox!

The dying one offered me more life than I offered that day.

There were other strange encounters during my visits to the Home for the Dying over the years. Sometimes the patients would sing to me. Sometimes they would try to share their food with me. And sometimes they would allow me to tend to their most intimate needs. Death and life intertwined in extraordinary ways.

Though most of us shun it, death is a necessary part of life. Life and death necessarily mingle together.

DEATH BRINGS LIFE

It was springtime in Spain when we set out on the Camino. After a long winter in Omaha, the freshness of a new season was a welcomed gift. How we had longed for the buds of life on trees, to see the new shoots of perennials. Along the road, new life was appearing in colors of green, red, yellow and violet. But the trees and flowers wouldn't have bloomed without the darkness of winter. The darkness of winter is an invitation to death. In order for the trees to bear fruit in the spring, a part of them had to die the previous winter. "For everything there is a season . . . a time to be born and a time to die, a time to plant and a time to uproot" (Ecclesiastes 3:1-2). By dying in season, the plants of spring and summer provide nourishment for the new life that will appear in the following spring. Death brings life.

Humanity is not exempt from nature's cycle of life and death. Most of us accept that eventually we will die—when we are old and gray, and hopefully while we are peacefully asleep. But there are other deaths throughout our lifetime to which we are subject. At birth, we die to the comfort and ease of life in the womb. At adolescence, we die to the innocence of childhood. As adults even the most celebratory moments of our lives—when we move to a new home or city, when we take a new job or get married or have a child—bear vestiges of death and mourning of the lives we've grown accustomed to and must leave behind. At midlife we may grieve the fact that most of our life is behind us. Then in old age, our body and mind begin to falter. And in the Christian tradition, adult baptism offers profound imagery for death and new life; it is an opportunity to die to our old way of being.

Dying at these stages brings the opportunity of experiencing new and different aspects of life—as a baby, the comfort of a mother's breast; as a young adult, leaving home, the delight of passions and dreams and ambitions; at marriage, the wonder of sacred commitment to a human being of our choosing; and in our faith decisions, the mystery of connection to the God of the universe. In such moments we experience a kind of death, even celebrate it, because of the life that extends beyond it.

REDEFINING MARRIAGE

When Chris and I first got married, we were certain we would have children. Chris planned on having six—he is the oldest of six siblings and thought that was a good number. I also wanted children, but being a little more realistic of what it would require of us, I thought it wise we start with two and see what we could handle after that; being careful about not being outnumbered seemed to make sense to me. We were so inclined toward having children that, before we were married, Chris bought a small Indian dress for our first baby girl and a small Nepali jacket for our first baby boy. We still have them. On our honeymoon we made lists of possible names for our future children. Everyone who knows us knows that we love children. So people are usually surprised when we tell them we decided not to have any of our own.

We didn't make this decision hastily or impulsively. We made the decision after years of honest, soul-searching conversation with one another, prayer, fasting and seeking counsel from others. And being sensitive to the maternal instinct, Chris largely deferred to me in the final decision.

As I took inventory of my upbringing and the people in my life, at the time, I couldn't find anyone who had made a decision to not have children, unless they'd also made a decision for celibacy. It seemed to me that a woman's identity very much centered on her relationship to her husband and her children—perhaps even more so in cultures of the East and South. Even after fourteen years of marriage with no children, when I visit some countries I still get asked, "When are you going to have a baby?" And I'm told, "You should have a child." And always, one of the first questions I'm asked when meeting someone new in any culture is, "Do you have children?"

Similarly, women are often pressured to get married. At least in the conservative Christian culture of the United States, if a young woman post university is not engaged or soon-to-be, people start to get nervous. Common questions for a young woman are, "When are you going to get married?" and "Are you dating anyone?" Generally, young men are offered more margin in time before they are plagued with these inquiries. Further, single men and women (at least in the evangelical subculture) are often not nurtured well enough in how to be in relationships with one another as friends and coworkers. The pressure to be an object of potential marriage undermines the exchange of platonic friendship. And this carries over after marriage—men and women struggle to know how to relate to one another outside of marriage. Can we be friends? Or does our friendship have to ride on the coattails of the same-sex friendship of our spouses? Are we so untrustworthy and out of control that we can't exercise restraint in male-female relationships?

Though the tide is slowly turning, a lot of my young, single female friends struggle to make a life for themselves if it doesn't involve a solid prospect for marriage. One young woman was recently heard talking about all the home furnishings she will not purchase until it's time to register for her wedding—she was not even in a dating relationship. Other young women I know struggle to find personal inner drive and ambition for anything other than getting married and having children. If they start a career, it is sometimes commenced as temporary, until marriage. And many women have too easily given up their life ambitions once they do get married under the assumption that this is what a wife and mother is meant to do.

Now please don't get me wrong. I understand that marriage and conceiving and bearing children are some of the most extraordinary experiences a person can have—and in a lot of cases it rightly requires the sacrifices women make. I think marriage is a holy sacrament and I feel really blessed to be married to such an incredible man. And I esteem motherhood (and fatherhood) as one of the highest callings. But I've also come to realize that there can be more to life than being a wife and mother—contrary to what the conservative subculture may suggest. And not being married and not having children can actually be a very fecund thing to do, though traditional Christian teaching has guilted a lot of us into thinking it is our Christian duty to get married and be fruitful and multiply in the form of biological reproduction.

The identity struggle and role tension I see in young women today can be understood from a number of perspectives. Human development theory suggests something insightful for this discussion. According to Robert Kegan in his book *The Evolving Self,* there are six stages of human development: incorporative, impulsive, imperial, interpersonal, institutional and, when fully mature, interindividual.[6]

Contrary to prevailing conservative Christian opinion, human development theory suggests that we don't acquire gender roles inherently alone. Culture also plays a large part in shaping expectations for men and women. And in many cases, women are not nurtured for the institutional development stage. Instead of being encouraged socially, religiously and educationally to develop our personal interests, ideologies, strengths, skills and gifts beyond relationships, they are reared, trained and educated to remain in the interpersonal stage—forced to find identity in relationship to others. Men in contrast are generally afforded the opportunity to develop further into the institutional stage, encouraged to pursue their own interests, ideologies, strengths, skills and gifts toward contributing to society and, traditionally, toward "providing for the family." This easily explains why young men aren't plagued with the same tensions in relationships and regarding marriage and children, and why young women often struggle to develop their identity into the creative stage of institution.

It's the twenty-first century and we've come a long way in recognizing the equality of women and men. But we still have miles to go before women and men are both free to develop their fullest potential, liberated to make free choices that connect to their deepest selves. For some men that might mean that being a homemaker would be the truest expression of who they are, but the pressures of society and culture don't typically allow that as an option.

The most difficult and most mature stage in human development theory, interindividual, is usually a struggle for both men and women. But if one is nurtured through the interpersonal and institutional stages of development, they can also find their way into the interindividual stage where mutuality is more possible: fully actualized men and women expressing themselves through a lovely exchange of persons, where giving and receiving is met with grace and appeal.

Having been reared well for the interpersonal stage, it was an earth-shattering proposition to consider choosing to not conceive children. I really had to wrestle with what it meant to be a woman. If being a woman means being defined in relationship to others—primarily husband and children—and I deny having this most sacred experience, then am I still a woman? I'm married. I can check that off my list. But what does it mean to be a woman if I don't have children? I would imagine that some women who, due to biology, cannot bear children go through similar daunting questions, as well as some women who are not married or are wrestling with the consideration of opting not to marry. If the woman is not Catholic or Anglican, she's really in a quandary since other Christian faith traditions do not offer an esteemed celibate option for people of either sex.

Making the decision to not have children meant I had to die to some of the false parts of myself that wanted to be connected, understood, accepted, and free of judgment and criticism. And most importantly, I had to die to the experience of ever conceiving a child, giving birth, and having reflections of Chris and me to enjoy and cherish for the rest of our lives. Not an easy decision. Not an easy death. There was necessary grieving and mourning involved.

But being available to a world of children who long for the same opportunities I would give my own was both the motivation for and the fruit of my decision. Because of this decision, in addition to being in relationship with a number of these children around the world, Chris and I get to spend our energies investing in an international community who will ensure provision and opportunity for children of poverty for years and years to come. And we get to enjoy and cherish a number of godchildren. Sure, these children aren't "our own," but we have a certain sense of responsibility to them nonetheless. We are committed to them to the extent of sacrificing the opportunity to conceive our own children. We are invested in their well-being, their personal development, their interests, their sadness, their hopes and their dreams.

So what does it mean to be "woman"? Certainly being a woman may include motherhood. There are plenty of happy mothers in the world. Yet what I had come to understand was that being a woman (like being a man) means to be free to be one's truest self (whether or not that includes parenthood). Being a woman (like being a man) means to be free of gender-role expectations imposed by family, religion, culture and society. Being free means that we are not defined by what we have, what we do or what others say about us.[7]

My decision to not conceive children is an expression of how the grace of God moved me from being *defined* by relationships to *having* relationships. A woman who chooses to have children can also achieve the same ends. Both decisions can be the truest expression of who we are. The point is not the outcome—being or not being married, or having or not having children. The point is to move from the interpersonal stage, where we are defined by our relationships, to the institutional stage, where we are free to uncover and be oriented by our ideologies—and to ultimately be free to be in mutual relationships of genuine interdependence (interindividual). Is this not the freedom Christ represented and offered through his friendships?

A woman's growth path often involves healthy differentiation that allows for separateness, while most men have a different experience. Being reared through the interpersonal stage to the institutional stage, they sometimes get stuck in being disconnected from relationships. The growth path for them involves differentiation that allows for connectedness. When men and women move through these paths of growth, they are able to experience relationships of mutuality.

REDEFINING CHRISTIAN FAITH

My decision to become Catholic was not any easier than my decision to not have children. Death was central to this decision, even in how the church designed the rite of initiation. In the early church, martyrdom was such a likely outcome of one's decision to become Christian that a three-year initiatory process was instituted so that one could contemplate the death they would endure by making this decision. We no longer have to wait three years—the Rite of Christian Initiation for Adults that I went through was a period of about eight months. (I added another four months or so onto the beginning of that time during my initial discernment.)

I was brought up to believe that Catholics weren't really Christians. But from an early age, because of a few Catholic friends, I was drawn to the liturgy and ritual of the Catholic faith tradition. As time went on, I received exemplary influence from Mother Teresa and the Missionaries of Charity as well as the Jesuits. But I didn't think leaving the evangelical tradition and becoming Catholic could ever really be possible for me. I didn't seriously consider it. However, after a few years of attending a Jesuit parish I began to take more seriously the prospect of conversion—turning from one way of expressing my Christian faith to another.

When sabbatical ended, I returned to Omaha and went back to my neighborhood parish, St. John's Catholic Church at Creighton University's campus. During the first Sunday mass I attended after my return, I was overwhelmed with emotion. I should tell you that I'm a "feeler." On the Myers-Briggs or Kiersey Temperament Sorter, I rank an F for "feeling." I filter the world through my emotions, and contrary to the rational mind, as a feeler it *is* possible to make decisions based on feelings. It's the primary way we feelers take in and process information. It's quite a remarkable way of interacting with the world. It took me years to accept the feeling part of me— perhaps because in a male-dominated world, the rational mind tends to be elevated as superior, and emotions are seen as inferior. A friend of mine actually said to his soon-to-be-bride when they were sorting out a conflict, "The rational mind is superior."[8] I remember, in college, being at a church service and going forward to the altar (we feelers can often be found at the altar) pouring out my heart to God, tears streaming down my face. The pastor quietly came to me and talked with me for a few brief moments. I apologized for crying and he said, "Never apologize for your tears. Some of us wish we could cry and can't. Your tears are a gift." I've never forgotten that.

So here I was, back at St. John's after being away five months. I gazed at Jesus on the cross and had this overwhelming sense that I had come home. The feeling was that I could find an ecclesial home for my soul (a phrase Chris so eloquently offered me in observing my conversion) in the Catholic tradition. And the invitation seemed to be that becoming a full part of the church with its sacraments and traditions would aid me in continued growth, transformation and intimacy with God. I had already stumbled my way into the contemplative tradition; and no other Christian faith tradition could cradle and nurture the contemplative part of me like the Catholic Church could. As I meditated on the cross, I knew that—for me—joining the Catholic Church would mean greater intimacy with Christ. Realizing this, how could I *not* become Catholic?

But in making this decision I would have to answer to my husband, father and countless Protestant friends—relationships that I often used to let define me. This was an opportunity once again to put to death parts of my false self that wanted to be understood, accepted and free of judgment and criticism. Whether viewed from a psychological perspective or a spirituality perspective, "The self truly dies to the self that was, and the new self that emerges is a kind of rebirth."[9] In the dying I was promised new life, but I couldn't know beforehand what that life would be like, and I had to trust that there would indeed be fruit from such a decision. "I tell you the truth, unless a kernel of wheat falls to the ground and dies, it remains only a single seed. But if it dies, it produces many seeds" (John 12:24).

So I counted the cost, found solidarity with the saints who went before me—and gave their very lives for their decision—and invited key people from my community into discernment. At one point during this season of discernment an article of mine was published in our community's quarterly journal, *The Cry*. In that article there was a photo of memorabilia from the Camino: my boots, walking stick and a rosary. A family member, after having seen the photo, asked my parents, "Has Phileena 'crossed over'?" News of my decision to become Catholic would not be easy or acceptable to a number of people in my life. My father and I had several very difficult conversations—the fruit of those has been greater understanding between us. Whereas before I was somewhat afraid for him to know the real me, I took the risk and invited him in, and he has faithfully stood by me. Other fruit and life has come and is coming from the decision. One of the greatest is unity among believers. Barriers of self-righteousness and judgment are brought under scrutiny when people who have known me for decades are forced to reconcile their condemnation of Catholicism with their appreciation for my faith.

Decisions that stand in opposition to the status quo are not for the faint-hearted; they require courage, honesty and risk. These kinds of decisions release us into our destiny. Abundant life awaits each of us, but we must die to obtain it. The challenge is to understand which part of us must die and which part is dying to be raised to life. Until we have grown sufficiently in self-knowledge, it is difficult—if not impossible—to distinguish the false self from the true. I had to die not only to the status quo but to repressive attachments that shackled me in a posture of inferiority and subordination so that I could live and reflect the truth of who God made me to be. This meant dying to my old way of being so that I could live into the responsibility of proper self-assertiveness.

In order to make the decisions to not conceive children and to join the Catholic Church, I had to die to traditional views of what it means to be a woman; and I had to die to religious paradigms and gender ideologies that threatened my very conscience against responding to God in a way that I knew to be right and good for me. For many men or people of power, what needs to die and what is dying to live will look rather different. I like the way Leo Tolstoy puts it: "The changes in our life must come from the impossibility to live otherwise than according to the demands of our conscience not from our mental resolution to try a new form of life."[10]

For many traditional women or persons of imposed powerlessness, the invitation to die is all the more problematic. From a human-development-theory approach, traditional teaching of self-sacrifice and nonassertiveness when one is transitioning from the interpersonal to the institutional stage only serves to repress one from reaching her or his full potential—or the abundant life of which Jesus so often spoke. Teaching that emphasizes assertiveness, empowerment and self-development aids the transition. I think this is why men traditionally make this transition with fewer impediments. Historically, in most cultures, boys are afforded this support while girls receive a message that reinforces subordination, dependence and self-effacing, which traps them in the interpersonal stage and prevents them from progressing to the institutional stage. Under these circumstances, girls too often grow up to be women without a proper sense of self to freely sacrifice. Rather than force women to choose between self-preservation and the church, can we not imagine a community of Christ where all are free to grow and develop into their full selfhood and unique destiny as people created in the image of God? Why on earth do we want to repress in the institution (the church) what is meant to reflect the reign of Christ?

All of this brings the message of the gospel to new light. Just how exactly are we to understand Christ's invitation for us to die? In view of what we now understand of the human psyche and development, this is not such a straightforward invitation. It requires an incredible degree of faith, trust and surrender so that we can understand the life in us that is called to die and the life in us that is dying to live.

Theology and psychology are not mutually exclusive; each informs the other. Together they enlighten us and help us understand what it means to be human and what it means to be a person of faith. The gifts of psychology and human development theory have given me a great appreciation and understanding for the teachings of Jesus. Through the lens of these disciplines, Christian transformation is tangible.

Remember the caterpillar in its cocoon and the long process of waiting? To live into the new life of a butterfly, the ways and existence of the caterpillar have to die. Can you imagine the absurdity of a butterfly trying to crawl and inch around like a caterpillar, rather than taking flight on its expansive wings? Death of the old caterpillar is necessary to live into the life of a butterfly. And like nanoscience revealed through its tiny microphones on the chrysalis, death is distressing. The artist in the *Studio 360* report said, "It is not so easy to become a fabulous being." The process of transformation requires an agonizing death of the old reality.

Immediately after my niece Claire was born she began to quietly moan—continuously. The doctors and nurses looked her over, put her under a lamp and examined her. After several moments when she would not stop moaning and whimpering, the nurse said, "She's lamenting." They actually have a medical term that explains this phenomenon—"lamenting." Claire was in mild distress. She was mourning. Exiting the body of her mother was no easy thing for this little one. She was mourning the familiarity and comfort of the womb. But leaving existence in the womb was absolutely critical to living the life of baby Claire. It's absurd to imagine a baby never leaving the womb. To live and grow into the fullness of who we are, we must move on no matter how painful and distressing it may seem at the moment. Death in varied forms is necessary.

I can't imagine what it is like for trees that succumb to the measured, arid process of autumn and winter. Slowly, slowly the tree dries out; the leaves begin to turn color, losing their life. Their death is imminent. And surprising to most of us, the beauty displayed in the changing colors of the leaves is a sign of their death. They are dying. But oh, isn't it beautiful? What's to be feared in such beauty and promise of new life in the springtime? And witnessing the birth of a baby! There's nothing like it! It's magnificent! But like Claire reminded me, the beauty of her birth required lamentation. And the caterpillar—can you imagine its experience in the chrysalis? The throngs of people visiting the Butterfly Pavilion at Omaha's Henry Doorly Zoo demonstrate our fascination and intrigue with the process of distress these creatures go through—an indispensable anguish to becoming their astonishingly exquisite self.

THE PASCHAL MYSTERY

In my awakening experience, I opened my eyes and, in some ways, saw myself for the first time. I saw that I was living in a posture of gender subordination that reinforced a perception that not only was I less than my male counterparts, but my sole purpose and design was to serve their interests. Prior to awakening, I didn't realize this was my self-perception; now I saw it for what it was. With eyes wide open, if this was who I was, then I wondered who God was—a God portrayed by people in my world from a very young age as the one who established this very order of nature in which male is superior, independent, autonomous and afforded a grand display of opportunity; and female is inferior, dependent, defined in relationship to others and offered limited opportunity (opportunities defined and provided for by her primary relationships). Who knew that a feminine awakening could include being confirmed into another patriarchal tradition? My decision to join the Catholic Church can only be understood within the paradox of God—a God who often dumbfounds us by choosing "the other."

Waking up to this state of affairs is one thing. Longing for something else propelled me forward. But it wasn't long before darkness set in and death was inevitable. It would take time for the life within me to come to fruition.

Jesus affirmed that abundant life requires a process of dying. The spiritual journey begins with a narrow way and carrying a cross—a symbol of our death. Jesus said,

> You who wish to be my followers must deny your very self,
> take up your cross—the instrument of your own death—
> every day, and follow in my steps. If you would save your
> life, you'll lose it, and if you would lose your life for my
> sake, you'll save it. What profit is there in gaining the whole
> world if you lose or forfeit yourselves in the process? (Luke
> 9:23-24)

This is the Teacher who invites us to die—daily. For a people
who flee from death, who can embrace such an invitation? Do we
cower from the pain that carrying our cross might impose? Do
we trust the one who claims he is the way? Can we follow him, no
matter what it might cost? Do we believe his way truly is the way
to life? Do we believe the narrow way that means our death will
ultimately lead to our being fully alive? The spiritual journey is
an invitation to identify with Christ in his paschal mystery.

The paschal mystery—Christ's passion, death and resurrection—is a mystery of participation for us. Christ's identification
with humanity and his suffering, death and resurrection provide a
way for us to make sense of our lives and find redemption. The
cliché that "Jesus saves" is not something to write off as a childish
belief. Jesus' salvation act in history is a mystery for us to enter
today—Jesus has made a way for us to receive fullness of life and
experience the love, growth and freedom that we long for.

Catholic priest and author Ronald Rolheiser explains the paschal mystery in four phases that relate to the events of Jesus' last
days on earth and the coming of the Holy Spirit. By his description
we can see the stages of redemption that we are invited into by
identifying with Christ's mystery:

Passion and death   the loss of life
Resurrection   the reception of new life

| Ascension | the refusal to cling, as ascending beyond the old life |
| Pentecost | the reception of new spirit for the new life[11] |

During sabbatical I began to reckon with my own passion and death. I began to understand that there were parts of me that had to die. I was in fact losing a part of my life. In seasons of death, we can take comfort in knowing we are not alone. We are like the residents in Mother Teresa's Home for the Dying—they are dying but they are not alone, and that makes all the difference. In our dying too, we are not alone. We are accompanied by Christ. Through his passion and death he has identified with us and made a way for us to identify with him. The act of dying might be the most profound way in which we can identify with God. Episcopal priest and author Cynthia Bourgeault says, "You do not die on a cross *in order* to 'set up' the resurrection; you die on a cross because the willingness to give it all away is itself the original and ultimate creative act from which all being flows."[12]

The season of Lent in the church calendar has become one of the most meaningful seasons of the year for me. Lent is the long period of forty days prior to Easter and the celebration of the resurrection of Christ. It is observed through prayer, fasting and almsgiving. As we spend forty days in intentional reflection on the passion of Christ, a grace is opened up for us to take inventory of the passion we may find ourselves enduring. Through keeping Lent, Jesus' life and suffering become tangible companions in the difficult seasons of life and death we endure. We receive the graces of patience and long-suffering. And we uncover a new hope in the promised resurrection. The paschal mystery is a grace-filled invitation to be accompanied by God through awakening, longing, darkness and death. The mystery reminds us that death does not have the last word.

Fruit comes from dying, like the grain of wheat; new life comes from death.

WE WANT THE FRUIT BUT RESIST THE DYING

The process a tree goes through during the changing seasons from autumn to winter is slow and dry and brutal to the leaves. The leaves are forced to die. Does the tree resist? Or does it surrender to the process in the hope that new life will come in due time?

We want the fruit, the new life, but we resist the dying. Death is the culmination of darkness. During a season of darkness, I wrestled with God, trying to hold on to that which needed to die—my preconceived notions of who God is and who I am. Much of what my identity had been based in was being shattered and I fought to hold onto the crumbling pieces—having no guarantee of who I'd be without my false-self security blanket. The burning away (purgation) of my false self was a horrible experience. At times, I didn't understand what was happening to me. I was sad and disoriented, and all seemed dark. I was losing grasp on who I was. I questioned all of my life's decisions, wondering which of them had been connected to my true self and which had been motivated by my false self. I was just trying to keep my head above water in the sea of darkness when everything about my identity seemed to be fading away.

Looking back, I can see that this was a necessary purging. To be free to live into my true self I had to examine and reckon layers of my identity that were oriented in a false way. I had very little control over this earth-shattering process. I had consented to the journey. I willed to embark on it, but like the Camino, if I wanted to reach the destination I would have to succumb to the pain and anguish that would get me there. After a considerable amount of time in purgation, death sets in. False self-perceptions and false God-concepts die. But purgation isn't enough. The purging season is a time to separate the false from the true. Once the separation is complete, the false-self stuff has to die to make room for truth. Death provides nourishment for the true self seed of life that has been incubating in darkness.

The gifts and perspective I had to offer from my true self had to be nourished on the dead leaves and mulch of childhood lies and attachments that suggested that I was less than equal, that I was to remain hidden and that my destiny was determined and limited by my relationship to others, particularly men. No longer could I define myself by relationships; I had to die to that misrepresentation of my true self. Christ was resurrecting my passions and calling forth feminine strength in the dried bones of my diminished sense of self.

But with these deaths came a lament, for my identity was intricately tied to these false perceptions and attachments. Like a drug user, I was addicted to the gratification these attachments afforded. Their effect was momentarily satiating. I craved the affection and esteem these paradigms offered me. And yet, like drug addiction, the very thing I craved was killing me. I longed to be free.

DEATH LEADS TO TRANSFORMATION

In my community, we are blessed to be in relationship with children and young people on the margins of society trying to survive on the streets without a traditional family; for various reasons they either do not have parents or no longer live with their parents. In their resourcefulness they attempt to re-create family through a network of loyal friendships on the street, as well as exploitative relationships. Drug abuse, indiscriminate sex and crime fill these children's world. The adage "You can take a kid off the streets but you can't take the streets out of the kid" is proven over and over again.

Transformation is not easy. Having been abandoned by their parents, either literally or emotionally, our friends have learned to survive on their own and rarely depend on anyone. They are hardened and so, instead of being free to be honest with their real developmental needs and trust another to tend to those, they turn to a quick fix through drugs, sex and crime. It's easier to go into survival mode, rather than to do the hard work of risking trust and relationship. They have reasons not to trust and their hearts have been broken too many times. They often believe the lies that they are unlovable, unworthy and unequal. They often believe they deserve nothing more than the repressive life they've been handed.

Like many of my young friends suffering on the urban streets of the Majority World, I had been living a lie about who I was. And living into the truth of my identity would be easier said than done. The old and new were in conflict with one another, and like oil and water, they wouldn't mix. Like the log of wood that St. John of the Cross so aptly describes, death has to come to the log of our false self so that our true self can burn brightly. After a considerable amount of time in purgation—that wrestling match between the darkness we inhabit and the longing we're cultivating—death sets in.

Death, a life-giving surrender.

The seed of life incubating within me promised another way of being. Like the crimson red, monthly blood flow demanding to be recognized, being me meant being unashamedly feminine, assertive, fecund, confident and bold, purposeful and passionate. Could this promise really be actualized in my life? Like the caterpillar, in order to live into this new, truer essence, the old way of being had to die. At the point of death, what dies, dies. Gone. No one knows for sure what, if anything, will come from the death. That's what makes dying so terrifying. Maybe the tree won't bear any leaves next spring. Maybe the caterpillar will die in its cocoon and never become a butterfly. Wouldn't it have been better to have not entered the cocoon but remained in a caterpillar's existence? Maybe slavery in Egypt was better. How do we know there's really a Promised Land? Maybe the baby won't live if it comes out of the womb. Do we risk pregnancy?

There are no guarantees. New life, growth and transformation are risky endeavors. The spiritual journey requires faith and trust. If we want resurrected life, at some point we have to succumb to our crosses and die.

5   TRANSFORMATION

Your joy is your sorrow unmasked.
And the selfsame well from which your laughter rises
was oftentimes filled with your tears.
And how else can it be?
The deeper that sorrow carves into your being,
the more joy you can contain.
Is not the cup that holds your wine
the very cup that was burned in the potter's oven?

KAHLIL GIBRAN, *THE PROPHET*

ALONG THE CAMINO, CHRIS AND I laughed and cried, we celebrated and we grieved. Some of the most vulnerable places in our souls emerged to be embraced by the all-consuming grace of God. And by that grace we kept moving forward. Many days our packs weighed us down and the pain in our bodies intensified. Inevitably, the harder it got to keep going on any particular day, the more our gaze turned downward. Staring at our boots on a dirt path was rarely motivating. At those times we would encourage one another to keep our heads up, to keep looking around us and before us. In this way we abandoned ourselves to our surroundings, to the horizon and to God, and found the strength to keep moving.

Often throughout our journey, I returned to the thought that pilgrimage is not a round trip. We begin at one point and end at another. We don't go back and retrace or relive our steps. Each moment is lived and let go. By way of El Camino de Santiago, we made a passage through time and into the next season of our lives. As we walked, our pilgrimage became a transformative passage to new life. Starting out, I had no idea that such a journey would mean so much pain. Neither did I anticipate the depth of joy and love we would experience. Like the Lebanese poet Kahlil Gibran expresses, our joy ran as deep as our sorrow. The pain and trial we experienced carved space in us for untold joy. Indulging our senses with the beauty of creation all around us, finding encouragement in the company of ancient and modern pilgrims, and experiencing many Spanish culinary pleasures filled the empty and dry places in our hearts that had emerged over the past thirty years of our lives. As we walked and embraced both the pain and the joy, we were being changed.

FROM DEATH TO NEW LIFE

Like a caterpillar in her cocoon, or a germinating seed, I was changing—undergoing a transformational regeneration of my soul. After months of sitting with an awakened sense of self, experiencing an internal death and learning to simply be, I was changing. These changes in me were both now and not yet—this is the reign of God spoken about so often in the Gospels. At times, Jesus spoke of the kingdom of God as if it is something to come. At other times he spoke as if it is at hand. Some changes had occurred in me, and others were imminent because of what had been set in motion within me, but living into the transformation would take time.

Most butterflies complete their metamorphosis or maturation within thirty to forty days, but human maturation takes much longer. We have long childhoods. This isn't something to be ashamed of, but aware of. Being ignorant or oblivious to this fact leaves us neglecting a natural phase of life. We force maturity before we have actually reached that stage in our awareness, enlightenment or development. Our culture certainly promotes growing up too fast. Children are confronted with adult choices on a daily basis through mass media and marketing. The retail industry has limited child-style clothing options but provides adult clothes in little sizes. Beauty and fashion industries entice preteens to apply makeup and dress sexy. Visual and audio content meant for mature adults is forced into the worldview of the preadolescent. The days are nearly gone when a kid can be a kid. The time needed at the childhood phase is sorely compromised.

On the flip side, our culture *prolongs* adolescence in the lives of adults, delaying our timely maturation. Juvenile programming is cloaked as adult entertainment. Some grown men can't pull away from their Xbox long enough to be a husband and father or general contributor to society. They are numbed into a virtual reality of perpetual childhood. Our culture also reinforces delayed maturation in the lives of women. The fashion and makeup, fitness and cosmetic surgery industries scream at women to stay young.

We are either tempted to grow up too fast or to sedate our growth and transformation. We are a discontented species who seem to resist the natural rhythms of our life and growth. If only we knew what was good for us. We can learn a lesson from the butterfly. She responds to the invitation for change not a moment too soon or too late, and submits to the process, no matter how difficult and painful it might be.

Fascinatingly, once the butterfly cracks its chrysalis—which takes about five minutes—it waits. It doesn't spring forth and take flight immediately. The newly transformed insect requires about

ten minutes to inflate its wings to full size—fluids from the abdomen are forced into the wings to inflate them—and then the butterfly rests for two to eight hours, allowing the wings to harden
before it is able to take flight.

Likewise, the transformation I longed for months to experience
just wouldn't happen overnight. It was like physical conditioning
in pilgrimage: transforming the body to endure the feats of walking five hundred miles happened gradually, day by day. Even once
I emerged from a long darkness and death, like the butterfly I
seemed to perch on the outside of my cocoon and wait a bit longer.
All the while, an inner strength was circulating through me, hard-
ening the modifications within to ensure my ability to live into
those changes and take flight.

CHANGE DEMANDS REST

Like butterfly wisdom, sabbatical introduced me to the spirituality
of rest and the crucial connection of rest to transformation.

> As I sit in the screened-in back porch of the "Rose Cottage"
> the soft rain is penetrating the dry and weary land of Dur-
> ham. North Carolina has been in a season of drought and so
> the rain is a long-awaited gift. Earlier this afternoon as I was
> in prayer, I heard the rain begin to fall. I transitioned and
> took my prayer outside to receive the baptism of fresh au-
> tumn, life-giving water. Each day on sabbatical is a gift. How
> could we have known how spiritual rest could be? My days
> are filled with renewal for my body, mind and soul.[1]

It was a little difficult to pull away from my community for several months to enter sabbatical. *What would become of me and my
marriage outside our usual context? What would come of my relationships? How could I ensure that my friends and I would grow
closer and not further apart during this absence?* Fear reared its
head and I struggled to let go. *Could this solitude create an empti-*

ness within us that would prove to be the source of our togetherness?
Detachment and solitude were necessary parts of this season of
rest and would prove to be essential elements for transformation.

The first month of sabbatical at Duke was transition—spiritually, mentally, emotionally and physically. As the good Puritan
work ethic collided with sabbath rest, I spent time pondering and
crafting my "rule of life."[2] Thinking a rule of life would help me
make the most of sabbatical, I dutifully and diligently put together
my rule for rest. Though my intentions were good, I now chuckle
at the thought of how contradictory this effort probably was to
truly entering rest. I chalk this period of time up to *transition.* I had
not really been taught *how* to enter a long rest and, therefore, as I
plunged in I had to figure it out along the way.

Sabbath rest is in fact a "revolutionary act."[3] Like making pilgrimage, by receiving time and space to purposefully detach from
my active life, I was denouncing the compulsions that our technology-
driven, rhythm-defying modern society affirms and indeed demands. By withdrawing and ceasing, I was announcing something
countercultural and otherworldly. It would take time to adjust.

At first I found myself unable to be present to the moment, instead fretting that sabbatical would soon be over. In the darkness,
I wondered if I would be ready to enter back into my normal life. I
was feeling abandoned in the dark, questioning my call, my life
decisions, God's work in my life and my very self. Tilden Edwards
articulates well the questions that rose in my heart.

> Ceasing from work tests our trust: Will the world and I fall
> apart if I stop making things happen for a while? Is life really
> gifted and the Spirit moving through it, so that I can truly
> rest and taste this restful caring? Can I trust that this caring
> will be the bottom line when I rest, beneath all the suppressed
> and repressed sides of myself that are likely to rise when I
> relax my controlling reins? Is there truly a unique image of

God in me that is simply given and rises to obscure awareness in such spacious times, an image that is my deepest
identity? Is there really no such deep self in God, and does
everything really depend on my producing, asserting and
protecting a conscious, managing ego-self?[4]

Edwards also says that when we enter sabbath rest as an escape,
"Sabbath rest is never quite full, because there is a lurking dread that
we may run into something from 'the other side' that will destroy
it."[5] My journal entry during sabbatical describes this struggle:

> The constant passing of the hours and my focus on tomorrow
> threatened to rob me of present peace and rest. I am becom-
> ing newly acquainted with Time, being invited into a differ-
> ent quality of time from my normal life. Time is asking me to
> receive it as gift rather than enemy, and asking me to risk fac-
> ing my lurking doubts, fears and questions.
>
> Unfortunately, this does not happen overnight. This is a
> process of healing. This is living the redemption.
>
> Much like yoga, there are times when we accept a position
> that hurts a little and stretches us in ways of which we didn't
> know we were capable. It hurts, it challenges my limits and
> my patience, yet if I sit with that dull pain for a while it
> changes me. I may want to not experience that pain or I may
> want to cut it short, but then I would not reap its rewards.
>
> In life we sometimes wish our pain would not linger so
> long. But for our benefit there is a necessary season of sitting,
> walking, living in our pain. When we embrace our pain, own
> it, we let it transform us.
>
> "Pain is weakness leaving the body," Chris says remem-
> bering his days of football training. An oyster endures the
> pain of the pebble in its flesh and that pebble is transformed
> into a costly pearl. The pain Christ endured on the cross led
> to his conquering of death and resurrecting into new life.

His pain is salvation for the entire world.

I trust that my pain could also bring forth strength, priceless gifts and salvation for others. This is the paschal mystery that we are all invited into—living, dying and being resurrected to new life.[6]

The Jewish tradition of sabbath and sabbatical is a time for waiting on, resting in, receiving from and learning to delight in God. According to the Hebrew Scriptures, sabbath was a day of rest from work and activity in honor of God's seventh day of rest in the creation story. This was a most holy day and was intended to be distinguished as such. Sabbatical was a similar principle, but for a longer period of time—one year set aside every seventh year.

A day of rest set aside weekly and more extensive periods of rest throughout one's lifetime allow for an inner work in our soul that is otherwise left neglected. Sometimes, these restful moments take the shape of apparent movement like pilgrimage, a hike in the mountains, a long walk or even the labyrinth prayer.[7] In these ways, though we are active we are actively *disengaged* from our normal activity. Other times, rest demands a quality of stillness. Rhythms of activity and stillness allow us to make music of our lives.

Our modern society abandoned the more natural rhythms of agrarian culture long ago. And with modernization has come ignorance to the body and soul's natural needs and rhythms. In previous times, not so long ago, our people were rooted to a time and place that lent itself to the more natural ways of being human with our bodily needs and rhythms for work and rest. Before the wonder of the automobile, our ancestors were fairly localized—they couldn't travel far very fast, so they didn't go far from home. Furthermore, our agrarian relatives were tied to the earth for their sustenance; they had to work the land. Any gardener knows you can't be away for long when you have plants to tend to.

My grandparents were farmers. Though they lived just forty-five minutes by car from me as a child, they rarely came to visit. They had cows to milk and chickens to feed and crops to tend to. They were relentlessly tied to their place in time. When the sun went down, they did too. And they would rise with it the next morning and live their life in connection to the living creatures all around them. Their home was quiet, peaceful, simple—much simpler than *Real Simple* magazine, a feeble attempt at reclaiming the value of simplicity in a complex, industrialized society. Achieving simplicity according to the popular magazine means stirring up a discontent in the reader in order to want something more—which leads to buying something more—in the false hope that all will be better once we've spent time calculating all these ideas, planning strategic points of action, purchasing the necessities that will "simplify" our lives—and then cluttering up our already overcluttered homes with yet one more foolhardy remedy to simplify our minds, hearts, homes and lives. And of course, we'll need to add this magazine to our long list of subscriptions in a lame attempt toward simplifying our lives to have more space, more time and more energy—whatever is left after the mass download of information through print, television, Internet, iPod, iPhone and BlackBerry.

I love the way Wes Jackson puts it in his book *Becoming Native to This Place.*[8] Jackson has spent more than thirty years taking on the modern agricultural industry, insisting it must change to sustain both our food production and ecosystem. He has a big dream and will die fighting for it. He's a person who will change the world. In his grand, broad-scope dream for revolutionizing the global agricultural industry, he makes a very simple point about being rooted in time and place. Jackson affirms that we are creatures of habitat with rhythms and connections to the natural world—meant to live in harmony with it, rather than in discord. But our modernity threatens that connection and harmony. In an attempt to regain our equilibrium, we build castles in the sky, sprawling retreat centers, spas and vacation packages, which become new loci for breathless acquisition and busyness. All our bodies and souls really need is a long walk in the woods or along the coast, getting back in touch with our habitat. Primitive agrarian cultures teach us something of the value of becoming native to our place—helping us to get back in touch with the elements of our own nature that thrive on rhythm and balance.

In our modern world, it is much too easy to overextend our limits toward activity and productivity. Stillness, solitude and silence are not valued today like they may have been for our ancestors whose days were filled with these qualities simply by the nature of their life's labor and limitations. We tend to see restrictions to activity and engagement as something to be avoided. But limitations and restrictions can be a grace for us. Within the context of our limitations, God can do for us what we cannot. The caterpillar can't make herself become the butterfly—that kind of change requires confinement, solitude, stillness and receptivity to something bigger than herself. This is how transformation is made possible. Remember, we cannot make ourselves grow; but we can choose to submit to or resist the process. And though much growth takes place in our active lives, all elements of creation are subject to contemplative stillness as an integral part of growth and transformation. The butterfly does not become the magnificent, colorful creature by a fury of activity. She submits to the confinement of the chrysalis—womb-like, tomb-like. She is still. She rests. She receives. She submits to a work more glorious than she could have ever conjured up for herself.

SABBATICAL: MY CHRYSALIS

Sabbatical prompted in me a posture like that of the caterpillar-come-butterfly. I entered my chrysalis by way of an extended period of time confined to a place that was strictly intended for rest and renewal. Sabbatical was a disciplined season of withdrawal, detachment, solitude, silence and stillness.

For more than a decade, Chris and I had engaged a world of poverty—children forced to be soldiers in West Africa, children abandoned because of AIDS in India, women and girls enslaved in the commercial sex industry, victims of war in Kosovo, children living on the streets in urban centers of South America. Wanting to respond to these people who had become our friends compelled me to give everything I could toward building an international community that would bear witness to a better world—a community that would emulate justice, peace, equality and opportunity, a community that would reflect the reign of Christ. In a world like ours where the work seems to never get done and there's always more to do, our community encouraged my husband and me to rest from this labor. It's sort of shocking, isn't it? In a world of extreme injustice and poverty, how could we stop serving and disengage from it all? There's so much to be done.

Leonardo da Vinci offers insight into the need for rest:

> Every now and then go away, have a little relaxation, for when you come back to your work, your judgment will be surer, since to remain constantly at work you lose power of judgment. Go some distance away because then the work appears smaller and more of it can be taken in at a glance, and lack of harmony or proportions is more readily seen.

Again, Mother Teresa teaches us. In her rules she established a rigorous schedule of service accompanied by a thoughtful period of regular rest—one day a week, one week a month, one month per year, one year in every six. Mother knew better than any of us that our labor on behalf of the poor is tireless. But she also understood the value of solitude, silence and stillness. Even throughout an active day of service in the life of a Missionary of Charity, every sister keeps to a routine of prayer interspersed throughout their workday. In Nirmal Hriday, amidst a sea of dying men and women, at particular hours in the day you will find the sisters withdrawing to pray in the upstairs chapel. Mother said, "We need to find God, and [God] cannot be found in noise and restlessness. God is the friend of silence. See how nature—trees, flowers, grass—grows in silence; see the stars, the moon and the sun, how they move in silence. . . . We need silence to be able to touch souls."[9]

And this kind of silence is more about an interior state than it is necessarily about the external. Mother's chapel is built facing one of the busiest streets in Kolkata. I've never been in that chapel when it's quiet. But the nuns who gather there still their minds, bodies and souls for regular, brief moments in their day—even amidst the sounds of blaring horns, diesel trucks and people calling out the sale of their wares. Rest, stillness, solitude and silence are all critical conditions to transformation in our lives and the world around us.

Work—Rest. Service—Prayer. Action—Contemplation. Life offers us the challenge of holding these essential elements of what it means to be human in tension with one another. One without the other leads to either pompous piety or frantic fury. The one who closes herself off from the world under the guise of "prayer" is at risk of becoming out of touch, irrelevant and prone to self-righteousness. In her "prayerfulness" she may succumb to judgment and superiority since she is not connected with the real lives of people around her. True prayer connects us with the compassionate Christ who connects us to all humanity and inspires us toward compassionate service.[10]

Similarly, the one who neglects contemplation is at risk of being motivated and driven by false-self compulsions. When one neglects giving attention to his interior life, he is not master of his house. His "programs for happiness" control him, and he goes through life unaware that his "service" is more truly frenetic activity. He is not only blind to the real needs of those he serves but to his own needs as well. True acts of service do not build up our egos but bring us into deeper solidarity with the poor, marginalized and victims of injustice, who compel us to prayer.[11]

Parker Palmer drives this point home:

> Too much of our action is really RE-action. Such "doing" does not flow from free and independent hearts, but depends on external provocation. It does not come from our sense of who we are and what we want to do, but from our anxious reading of how others define us and of what the world demands. When we react this way we do not act humanly.[12]

Our community had the wisdom to recognize the imperative value of rest in what had become a very intense bent toward service. Chris and I had leaned heavily into the question, "What can I do for God?" and neglected to regularly recognize our need to ask, "What can God do for me?" We were victims of the Puritan work ethic. We struggled to find people in similar fields of service who modeled sabbatical (rest) well. Chris and I entered pilgrimage and the season at Duke tenuously. The prospect of five months of detachment from work loomed over me and seemed more daunting than visiting former child-combatants in Sierra Leone. What in the world would I do with all the time?

And time was all I had. No obligations. No major responsibilities. The time given me amounted to a lot of waiting time. Waiting turned into longing. Longing mingled with darkness and death. The spiritual journey as a passage for growth and transformation was upon me. I didn't realize then during the long days of relative stillness in the Rose Cottage, as I sat in the darkness of my soul and felt abandoned by God, that everything I was experiencing was a part of the process of transformation. Like the caterpillar in her cocoon, I felt the distress and torment of my confinement. Everything seemed dark and I didn't understand what was happening to me. All I could do was succumb to the pain in my soul, try to grasp it somehow and try to understand it.

In my desperation all I could do was cry out for mercy.

As the weeks turned into months I found myself fragmented. Through prayer, purgation had the effect of separating my false self from my true self, and I was left in pieces. I remembered the Gospel stories about sick and disabled people wanting Jesus to make them whole, and this had never made more sense to me. I too wanted to be whole. And I was powerless to make that happen. This is a work of the Divine Physician[13]—the one I doubted then and still doubt at times. And yet when the uncertainty creeps in, all I have to do is look at the changes in me and I am brought to my knees at the wonder of my Creator, Savior and Friend. My priest once said, "The opposite of faith is not doubt, it's certainty." The essence of faith anchors me even in the midst of misgivings.

Transformation, which essentially involves healing, is a slow process. It is rarely full and complete in an instant. It takes time. And during that time, it demands cycles of awakening, longing, darkness and, yes, even death. All are crucial to this most sacred work in us. Being healed of that which shackled me and prevented me from being fully me took time and space for solitude, silence and stillness. You might enter a sabbatical expecting a kind of convalescence, but it wound up being more like rehab for me—lots of stumbling and frustration and even anguish. This is how it feels when you emerge from your cocoon as you begin to live into your true self—the person loved for who you are alone and not what you can do or be for others. During seasons of transformation we have to find our footing and let our wings harden so we can make the flight of our life. An intentional sabbath season made it possible for me to enter my chrysalis and submit to a metamorphosis of my soul.

I love how Tilden Edwards explains sabbath: "Sabbath rest . . . emphasizes trustfully relaxing into what already has happened and is happening for us in God's easeful grace."[14] Sabbath time is characterized by catching our breath, ceasing and freedom from compulsion. It is a deeper communion with God, our self and our community. Contribution through acts of service or work can more easily and purely flow from this communion. Apart from communion with God, our action is more likely a compulsive, anxious attempt at imposing our will on the world.

The gifts of sabbath are available to everyone, even if you are not able to receive a sabbatical. When kept mindfully and thoughtfully, any regimen of sabbath can create optimal conditions for soul-tending, growth and transformation. If we posture our lives through the lens of pilgrimage or the spiritual journey, all we have to do is open our eyes and find that we are in the grace-filled passage of transformation. At any given point in life we can find ourselves at various places: awakening, longing, darkness, death, transformation. All are prime moments to rest in the arms of God.

GROWING ACQUAINTED WITH GOD'S SILENCE AND LEARNING TO LISTEN

While I was at Duke, the difference between compulsion and communion became more apparent. God's easeful grace led me into a long, lingering experience of *being* as I've never experienced before. I read novels—lots of them. I read a history book on the sordid past of Durham's race and class division in an effort to root myself in the city in which I found myself living.[15] I prayed and meditated—more often than I ever had before. I gardened for hours and took long walks with no destination. I took advantage of being near the Atlantic Coast, spending a total of fifteen days by the sea in a matter of three and a half months. I enjoyed some creative cooking, going to shows with Chris, and sitting and having long talks in the outdoor hot tub with him. And I even enjoyed accompanying him to a couple of football games (he took full advantage of sabbatical and his love for college football, attending sixteen games over the course of four months). I lingered in the backyard hammock—reading and dozing. I walked through Duke Forest and marveled at the changing colors of the falling (dying) leaves. From day to day, I tried to reach deep down in my soul to discover what I wanted and needed, freeing myself of former compulsions to do and be that which I thought others wanted or needed of me.

At about the halfway point during my time in Durham, a much-needed rain began to fall after a long drought. The climate had been uncharacteristically hot for the autumn and with the rain came welcomed cooler temperatures. On the first day of the downpour, since I had no real agenda for the day (like most days on sabbatical), I abandoned all convention and went for a walk in the rainstorm. With all the determination of pilgrimage, my walk turned into a run until I could run no longer. The pink Rosie Thomas T-shirt I was wearing clung to my body, reminding me of the nakedness beneath that reflected my vulnerable soul. My soul longed to be exposed and embraced in grace and freedom. I was desperate for this baptism—more so than the relatively innocent nine-year-old who was baptized many years before. How my entire being needed the Water of Life that Jesus claims to be. The rain kept pouring down and I couldn't bring myself to go inside. It was as if all of creation were crying out for me to pay attention and be present.

So I walked to the neighborhood park and swung alone on the swing until my hips were sore from the child-sized seat. The previous few days, I had experienced the trials of soul-searching and I desperately wanted to hear from the Lord. I was weary of the darkness and longed for better days of full release and freedom. I cried out to God to speak to me. I told God how much I needed to know the comforting Presence. I felt so alone.

Though I wasn't able to hear God's voice in the way I was asking for it, at that moment I *heard* God's silence, and for the first time in a long time God's silence was okay with me. I no longer felt abandoned. I longed to worship. I was shedding compulsions for the liberating gift of communion. Love was growing in my soul—slow and feeble but it was there nonetheless—a love that longed to love regardless of what it received in return; a sign of transformation.

Later that afternoon, after reading a bit from my novel of the week and drinking my favorite pumpkin ale, I took a nap. When I awoke, I turned to the Gospel of St. John in prayer. As I entered *lectio divina*,[16] Jesus broke through the silence between us and spoke to me through the words of Scripture. The reading was from the story when Jesus healed the man at the pool of Bethesda.

> Here a great number of disabled people used to lie—the blind, the lame, the paralyzed. One who was there had been [disabled] for thirty-eight years. When Jesus saw him lying there and learned that he had been in this condition for a long time, he asked him, "Do you want to get well?" "Sir," [the disabled person] replied, "I have no one to help me into the pool when the water is stirred. While I am trying to get in, someone else goes down ahead of me." Then Jesus said to him, "Get up! Pick up your mat and walk." At once the man was cured; he picked up his mat and walked. The day on which this took place was a Sabbath. (John 5:3-9 TNIV)

Clearly I was that disabled person longing to be made whole on the sabbath. Jesus took compassion on me, noting that I had been in this condition for a long time. The past months of darkness had brought me to a greater realization of that very condition. For security's sake, I had clung all these years to my pitiful human condition filled with attachments and compulsions that weren't good for me—like being defined in relationship to others and succumbing to self-abnegation. As the darkness progressed over time, I was being invited to let go of this false security of self, not knowing what would be given in return. In those moments with the Scripture before me, as Jesus asked me if I wanted to get well, I was overwhelmed and wanted to shout, "Yes!" God had heard my cry for mercy. Having come to greater understanding of my personal human condition, I wanted nothing more than to be well, to be made whole, to be transformed.

One of the things I love about Jesus is that he never imposes himself on us. He always offers but never coerces. Time and again in the Scriptures we find Jesus confronting people with all kinds of ailments, but he doesn't force them into healing. As the noblest of all gentlemen, he asks what he can do for them and asks if they want to be well. Jesus never pushes us into something we're not ready for. Jesus is so patient with us. He leads us tenderly and jealously at times, but he doesn't force us into the next season of abundant life or healing. He asks us what we want of him. In those moments with Christ, I poured out my grief and sorrow over my condition and, by faith, received the transformation that I couldn't offer myself.

As my self-perception and understanding of what it means to be woman was being healed and transformed, so also was my perception of God. Early in sabbatical I had the sense that God wanted to reintroduce God's self to me. Since so much of my understanding of God was shaped by masculine influence, my understanding was limited. And the distance I felt from God was caused in part by this misunderstanding. If God is perceived as male and men are often overpowering and all-pervasive, then there's no room for me as a woman in relationship to God or men. But here was this revelation of God in Jesus who, as a man, doesn't overpower, overshadow or impose himself. Though Jesus could fill the space of the world and is certainly self-sufficient, he restrains himself with remarkable discipline and control to make room for the other—all others, all of his creation. And he doesn't stop there. Making room for the other, he invites us into a relationship of mutuality—giving and also receiving. Incredible. If the God of the universe can make room for me and receive what I have to offer, then certainly humanity can too—most notably, men. In Jesus we see the portrait of what it means to be the best of masculine humanity—powerful but free of ego, dominant but tempered, strong but yielding to others. He has nothing to prove and everything to give. He is a respecter of persons—he affirms that masculine and feminine are both divine reflections. In relationship to him there is enough space for all of us to live in mutuality, offering our gifts and influence to one another. Some feminists have a really hard time accepting that in the life of Christ God chose to be revealed as a man and not a woman. But when seen in this light, God's incarnation as man becomes an incredible grace to men and women alike.[17]

After months of transformative silence, I was able to finally listen. God was reintroducing God's self to me and holding up a mirror to my true self. Jesus had never been more appealing. Love was taking root in my heart as I embraced my femininity and the gifts I could freely give to the world.

6   INTIMACY

Someone is standing near

Who will wash away her tears

Someday when she's been found

Her scars will become a crown

KATE HURLEY, "HEY LITTLE GIRL"

INTIMACY IS THE STARTING PLACE, the posture and the goal of the spiritual journey.

From a place of intimacy, for our tenth wedding anniversary Chris gifted me the promise of walking the Camino. Intimacy guided us through all the preparations we made to embark on the journey together. Intimacy rooted us to the experience of suffering and enduring together thirty-three days of physical feats and emotional exploits. And by the end of our journey, we had achieved greater intimacy with one another. The Camino became for me an outward, tangible experience of an invitation to journey deeper with others, God and surprisingly with myself. As I grow to understand and embrace myself more fully, intimacy with others grows too. Embracing myself requires me to come out from hiding (self-abnegation, self-effacing). Intimacy is about knowing and being known. How can I be known if I remain in hiding?

On the Camino, my apparent physical "weakness" caused me to feel terribly inferior to Chris. Biologically he is stronger. He can walk longer and faster and carry more weight. I, on the other hand, couldn't walk as far or as fast, and I certainly couldn't carry as much weight. I thought this made me less, but as I emerged from hiding I came to recognize my differences as a gift rather than an inferiority or inequality.

In light of this, on the third day when we walked from Zubri to Pamplona—the infamous day known as the "Phileena Shuffle"—I experienced a deeper intimacy with Chris. In my vulnerability and humiliation, I came out of hiding and acknowledged my difference from Chris in what felt like weakness. I owned my limitations and my needs and presented them to Chris. "Chris, I can't walk that fast. I'm in a lot of pain. I'm slowing us down. I'm sorry." And Chris responded, "Bebe, that's why you should lead the way to-day." "What?! You mean you accept me in this condition? You embrace me as I am in my felt weakness? And in being me, in my femininity and in my difference I can lead us?" Tears flooded my eyes as I proceeded before him.

Struggling to accept myself in this one area was an opening to a sinkhole of self-perception that had drained my influence and contribution to the marriage and to other relationships and endeavors. Being honest with who I was in that moment and revealing that to Chris—instead of hiding, trying to "buck up," "take it" and pretend like I could keep up—and being embraced in such a loving way by Chris helped me find the courage to be more truthful and honest with myself *and* with Chris (and others) about who I am.

This was the beginning of greater intimacy with Chris and a new step in confidently offering more contribution and influence to the marriage. In what seemed like inferiority, weakness and something less valued, my femininity and my unique personhood was actually a gift. It was time I embraced myself more fully. Ne-

glecting to do so was not only detrimental to myself but could be
to to others as well. Though Chris does have a different orientation
and pace for life than I do, he admittedly is subject to overdoing it
and getting ahead of himself and those around him. When I offer
myself, my perspective, my needs and limitations to him, it can
often be surprisingly liberating for him too. Often, the very part of
ourselves that we are most embarrassed by or feel most vulnerable
about is the exact gift others need from us. Regardless, embracing
these parts of ourselves is crucial to intimacy.

The spiritual journey allows for space within us to be carved for
intimacy. Intimacy is about knowing and being known. But sadly
there are a lot of obstacles that keep us from achieving this most
necessary of human needs. "Programs for happiness" that our false
selves cling to threaten to prevent us from reaching our hearts' desires for intimacy. We seek power and control, affection and esteem or security and survival, and none of these pursuits leave us
fulfilled. At the end of life's journey, it doesn't matter what we
have, what we do or what others say about us. What will matter is
whether or not we are known and loved for who we are, and
whether or not we have known and loved our family and friends
well. This is why family and old friends are the dearest. They know
us—the good, the bad and the ugly—and they still love us. We
want to be known, and we want to know and love others well—
this is the truest success in life. Countless novels and films center
on this very theme: the estranged family member on his or her dying bed seeking relationship, intimacy—they want to be known,
forgiven, loved, or they want to have one last attempt at knowing
and loving their family better.

The spiritual journey is an invitation to know God and to be
known by God, which necessitates that one finds and knows one-
self. Intimacy is something that either saturates our life or leaves us
craving more. Awakening to deeper intimacy with God fuels the
growth of intimacy with others, and vice-versa.[1] When we pursue

intimacy and our awareness is heightened to our limitations in intimacy, we are en route toward growth and transformation.

In order to grow in the intimacy we long for, we must cultivate self-knowledge. Self-knowledge cradles intimacy. And to the extent that we grow in understanding our deepest self, we grow in relationship to others. Often, when we don't experience the intimacy we want in relationships, we point the finger at the other person or at God and focus on their shortcomings and why they aren't able to allow for intimate relationship. Though this can be true—some of the people in our lives are limited in their ability to be intimate in the way we may desire—often the key to being known and knowing others is knowing our self. When we dare to know our deepest self, with its sorrows and hopes, we encounter God who, in turn, invites us to greater enlightenment about our self and the world that we live in. In knowing and embracing our self, we find courage to offer our self to the world—most intimately to the people with whom we are in relationship. We are more inclined to put our self out there to be known when we are comfortable in our own skin. If we are hiding behind our "programs for happiness," our desire for intimacy will never be satiated. We have to come out from hiding—naked and vulnerable—look at ourselves in the mirror, embrace and celebrate the person we are. Then we are free to be known and to more truly know others. An intimate exchange can occur.

During this season of my soul, I realized that I was attached to the "program for happiness" of affection and esteem. As long as I generally did and said what I thought others wanted or needed from me, I would feel "loved," "accepted," "desirable." But living in this manner perpetuated a slow internal decay. I wasn't a human being fully alive, but in a sense was living only half of my life. The other half was in hiding and scared to come out for fear of being rejected.

Aren't there parts like that in all of us? We offer the world what

we think are our "presentable" parts, and we tuck away what we
think are less desirable to others. In this manner our egos are
stroked and we subsist on the sustenance of our "program for happiness." But it is a survival technique nonetheless, not an abundant, thriving life. It's more like a parasitic relationship between
our ego and false self. The ego feeds on our "program for happiness." The longer this goes on the more emaciated the true self
becomes. Learning to know and embrace myself was not easy for a
woman who was religiously and culturally inclined toward a posture of subservience.

The journey that my soul embarked on was made possible by a
divine invitation to intimacy. The pilgrimage that I choose to continue on is one that grows in ever-deepening exchanges of intimacy
with God, my family and friends and all of creation. Growing in
self-knowledge and self-embrace is a surprising experience of being known and embraced by God.

AN AUDACIOUS PRESUMPTION

Longing is about growing acquainted with the presence of God. Intimacy is about friendship and growing toward union with God.

Several years ago, I started to wonder: *If I lived in a society of
religious persecution and was imprisoned and could no longer read
the Scriptures or attend church, or if I had been born into a family
and culture that did not know Christ and could not tell me about
him, could I still know God? Can we only know God through the
influence of others, or is it possible for God to reveal God's self to us
in a more direct way? Is God confined and contained in the Holy
Scripture, in our church services or in others' interpretation and explanation of God? Is God only to be found in these places or does
God also really dwell within me? Is it possible to be acquainted with
God without the usual "filters"?*

These questions beckoned me into deeper intimacy with God. I
am reminded of the disciple Thomas and how he has gotten a bad

rap. You know the one—the disciple who said, "Until I put my hand in his wounds, I will not believe!" (John 20:25-31). Well, why is that so bad? I relate to Thomas in some ways. I am a skeptic and a realist. Like Thomas, I wanted to see, touch and embrace God. I wanted a more intimate exchange. Perhaps like Thomas I was calling God's bluff. "If you really are the Christ and have risen from the dead, prove it. Show me yourself. And don't stop there. Show me your wounds—the most intimate, pain-filled places in you."

Even in the most insecure and vulnerable moments of my soul's journey, I occasionally had the sense that I was not alone. In fact, I now understand those darker moments as some of the most intimate encounters with the wounds of Christ. The invitation to intimacy beckoned me toward growth and transformation, which meant also a redemptive suffering. The desire for intimacy guides us through all of the movements of the soul.

What does it mean to know God? Primarily, I have come to know God through the life of Christ. When I think about my desires to know Jesus I don't want to take someone else's word for the reality and divinity of Christ. I want to know him myself. I want to be so near him that I too can put my hands in his wounds. I've begged to know him and he has been faithful to make himself known in my life. In the words of the anonymous fourteenth-century author of *The Cloud of Unknowing*, there is a yearning for God within me, "a longing to see and taste [God] as much as is possible in this life."[2]

One of the most evident ways God has been made known to me is through my friends around the world living in poverty and suffering all kinds of horrors. One of the most compelling reflections I gained from time with our young friends in West Africa centers on the wounds of Christ. The civil war in Sierra Leone was just ending. Soldiers were being disarmed. Boys as young as five were gathered in from the combat zone and forced to turn in their weapons. Unable to return to their villages because of the atrocities they were forced to commit under compulsion from their commanders, the children resigned to whatever social welfare the government or NGO community could provide them. They were desperate to find a way to live in peace in a war-torn country.

During one of our times together, Chris shared with them the story of Thomas. He asked, "If the Scriptures are true and Jesus is the same yesterday, today and forever, and if after his resurrection he still had the wounds (they weren't healed over even though his entire body had been raised from the dead)—then wouldn't he still bear wounds today? And if so, then where are the wounds of Christ in the world?" Without hesitation one of our friends, a former child soldier, replied with eagerness as he pounded his chest, "We are the wounds of Christ."[3]

This understanding is one of the ways in which our community can celebrate suffering. We don't vindicate or sacramentalize suffering; we grieve it, but we can also embrace it as a lifestyle celebration. Let me explain. The perpetrator and perpetration of suffering are not excusable. But through Christ, companionship and hope are found in the midst of our suffering. And this is why we can celebrate it. Through suffering, the wounds of Christ are revealed, providing an invitation to intimacy with God. To the degree that we respond to the wounds, we experience intimacy with the One who suffered for us and bore *our* wounds. Drawing near to the wounds in our brothers and sisters around the world, while simultaneously acknowledging our own, allows for healing and transformation to take place. In this way we can understand the words of the Hebrew prophet Isaiah, "By his wounds we are healed" (Isaiah 53:5).

Knowing God can be a challenging endeavor for people who are inclined to limit reality to their senses, but people of all times and cultures strive to know God nonetheless. We experience life and relationships by our ability to see, hear, smell, touch and taste. Certainly we can know something of God through reflections of God. It's like knowing a fine painter whom we might never meet:

we can know something of her or him as our senses encounter their piece of art. Poets and artists of all kinds help us achieve this kind of encounter with God.

But rather than knowing something *of* God, how can we know God personally and intimately? Classic Christian spirituality helps us with this. God is beyond our faculties: reason, imagination, memory, feelings and will. Prayer that makes use of our faculties is known as *cataphatic* (or *kataphatic*) prayer. Cataphatic prayer corresponds with ordinary awareness and reinforces our unique egoic selfhood. It is wonderfully self-reflective. "I" is the center of orientation for this kind of prayer. It arises from the predominant way in which we relate to the world and to others.

By contrast, *apophatic* prayer does not make use of our normal faculties. It transcends our capacities for reason, imagination, memory, feelings and will. The center of orientation for this kind of prayer—by its very nature—is abandonment of self and attentiveness to God. But this prayer does make use of *different kinds of faculties,* faculties that we are less in touch with, faculties known as "spiritual senses." Engaging our spiritual senses is enhanced through apophatic prayer, which is usually characterized by intentional silence or meditation. By way of apophatic prayer, we grow in receptivity to and awareness of God who is indeed very personal and intimate with us. In this kind of prayer, we grow in openness to God introducing God's self to us, very directly. True aspects of God that have been told to us become infused in us through the posture of surrender and attentiveness: God is gracious, compassionate, merciful and forgiving. And the most predominant impression we are left with as we grow acquainted with God in apophatic prayer is that God is love.[4]

Songwriter Kate Hurley echoes the revelation of the God of love that the ancient writer of Song of Songs understood. God is love. And the love of God is all-consuming. The essence of intimacy is experiencing this all-encompassing love.

I am my Beloved's and He is mine
When I found the one my soul loves
I held on to Him
When I found the one my soul loves
I would not let Him go
Love burns like a blazing fire,
Like a mighty flame
Many rivers cannot quench love,
Many waters cannot wash it away
Love burns like a blazing fire,
Like a mighty flame
For love is stronger than death,
Its jealousy unyielding as the grave
Place me like a seal on Your arm
Like a seal over Your heart
Love is stronger than death.[5]

Because of Christ's passion, death and resurrection a way is made for us to pass from death to life, from death to love. Christ has identified with us and with intimacy has invited us into his passion, death and resurrection. For ultimately, no death we face is stronger than love. Though the suffering and death we experience throughout life can at times seem unyielding, love always prevails. It is love's jealousy that invites us into the pain of our suffering and invites us to die so that love might be born. The invitation is to fullness of life and love. That fullness comes at a cost. We must die to obtain it. The dying may feel like it will have the last word, but the truth is that love always has the last word. The poet Kahlil Gibran explains this well:

When love beckons to you, follow him, Though his ways are hard and steep. And when his wings enfold you yield to him, Though the sword hidden among his pinions may wound you. . . . And think not you can direct the course of love. For love, if it finds you worthy, shall guide your course.[6]

Love leads us and at times it may penetrate us so deeply that we feel as if we are being wounded. But that "wounding" is actually for our healing and transformation.

Cultivating intimacy with God is not so different from cultivating it with our spouse or our friends and family. Depth of intimacy requires knowing our self and being honest with our self and with the other. I realized this in new ways during sabbatical. There were parts of my relationship with God that I didn't really want to be honest about, as my journal reveals:

> As I'm learning to give voice to things personally and in my marriage, today I realized how I must do that in my relationship with God. During the past week I've wanted to come to God out of adoration and worship and praise and yet I haven't found much of that in my soul. That has scared me a little.[7]

The truth in my relationship with God in those moments was that I didn't feel anything toward God, except a sense of being abandoned. But I was afraid to be honest. Would God accept me in that condition? Can we be honest about our doubts that God exists? Can we go to God and be honest about not really feeling like worshiping or praising? Can we show up to an encounter with God just as we are? Or do we opt for keeping a distance from God because we would rather be distant than honest? Cultivating intimacy with God in this season of my soul required honesty. I would show up in faith or reach out to God in faith, but in all honesty too, I acknowledged that I didn't know if God really existed, and if God did, I doubted God cared.

Henri Nouwen explains the role that doubt plays in intimacy:

> The [person] who never had any religious doubts during his college years probably walked around blindfolded; he who never experimented with his traditional values and ideas was probably more afraid than free. . . . But he who did, took a

risk . . . the risk of being alienated from his past and of becoming irritated by everything religious, even the word
"God." The risk even of the searing loneliness which Jesus
Christ suffered when He cried, "God, my God, why have you
forsaken me?" . . .

We can discover, with pain and frustration, that a mature
religious [person] is very close to the agnostic, and often we
have difficulty in deciding which name expresses better our
state of mind: agnostic or searching believer. Perhaps they are
closer than we tend to think.[8]

Though I feared being honest about my doubts in God, I was
learning that doubt does not stand in opposition to faith. Like my
priest said, "The opposite of faith is not doubt but certainty." In
fact, doubt is at times a necessary element to growing in faith. Being honest about my doubts and fears strangely brought me nearer
to God.

EMBODIMENT LEADS TO INTIMACY

It was on a day of that kind of honesty that my walk—in the steamy
North Carolina rain—turned into a run. In my drenched, vulnerable, embodied truthfulness I encountered God. God's silence
broke through to me and I experienced an intimate exchange. This
was an intimacy of embodiment. In relationship with a God whom
we struggle to grasp with our senses, actions of embodiment—
being present in our body as well as our mind—are extremely important. Sadly, Western culture has so prized the mind over the
body that the two have been divorced in much of our Christian
experience.

Western culture has historically segregated the life of the body
from the life of the mind, creating a dichotomy in which the
mind's work is given value and the body's work is disregarded or
actively devalued. This bias is an imposition on Christian his-

tory, which gave as much attention to the body as to the mind, developing spiritual practices such as pilgrimage, labyrinth prayers, genuflection, the sign of the cross and other embodied prayers. These kinds of practices, in addition to reading and intellectual reflection, are helpful for embodying our faith and growing in intimacy with God. We all have practices of embodiment; some of us just need to connect those to the One who made them possible.

I like to pray in the same chair; it's become a sacred place for me to embody my prayer. I experience embodiment every time I listen to Sergei Rachmaninoff's "All Night Vigil." I remember being at the Rose Cottage, with a fire in the fireplace and the orchestra sounding through the speakers, fully present in the moment and in the wonder of the music. In those moments, intimacy with God was tangible.

I also like to sit on a quiet, empty beach and watch the tide roll in. Yet sometimes it's incredibly difficult to be fully present—can you imagine? In the grandeur of the expanse of the sea, earth and sky, how can it be hard to be attentive and fully there? This is the problem: we are fragmented—our mind, body and soul have trouble coming into harmony. We have so overemphasized the mind in our Western experience that we are always in our heads.

Because we in the overdeveloped West have become so accustomed to privileging the mind over the body, disciplines of embodiment can be intimidating and even perplexing. My friend David went to yoga for the first time with another friend. Realizing David's uneasiness and anxiety going into class, his friend said, "Dude, you've got to get out of your head and into your body." Exactly—though perhaps more accurately it would be, "Dude, bring your mind in harmony with your body."

Going to confession can also be an act of embodiment. The action of taking our body to another to confess sin is a demonstration of our desire for intimacy with God. Realizing our sin, we recognize the ways in which we are separated and take steps toward intimacy.

As I prepared for my first confession in the Catholic Church, I was encouraged to think about themes in my life that separate me from God, myself, others and creation—contrary to the misperception that I would have to bring thirty-five years worth of a laundry list of sins to confess. It didn't take very many moments of meditation to know what my confession would be. As I met with my priest, I waded through tears and deep-felt emotion and confessed the sin of self-abnegation. It was one of the most intense experiences in my spiritual journey. I kept looking at the crucifix on the wall before me in the office. (That's right, I met face to face with my priest in his office—not in the mysterious, dreaded cubicle most often depicted in movies, though that could have been arranged as well.) As I gazed on the image of the Christ hanging on the wall, I was overcome by the impact of sin; even now as I think about it, the emotion fills my heart. Succumbing to self-abnegation —hiding, neglecting responsibility for my truest self, living out of response to what I thought others needed or wanted from me— had the direst consequences on my relationship with God, myself, others and the world. In the presence of my confessor I realized how this sin caused massive separation in my life and in the world around me.

What made this confession even more painful was that in my sin I thought I was doing the right thing. I thought my posture and attitude was a godly one. I thought I had been living as a good Christian woman. It was a confusing moment of enlightenment, as you can imagine. But now that I was confessing my sin, the feeling of being known was more tangible and the depth of intimacy in my relationship with God more possible. Christ's words on the cross touched me to my soul's core: "Abba forgive them. They don't know what they are doing" (Luke 23:24). At the moment of this confession I realized the devastating effect of my sin, while at the same time I realized that when I committed the sin, I didn't know what I was doing. What compassion of Christ! As he received the direst effects of the sin of humanity—through crucifixion—he could see that the people truly didn't know what they were doing. In fact, they thought they were doing the right thing.

A God who sets rules to follow and punishes those who break them no longer seemed real in light of the grace and revelation I experienced through confession. Suddenly, sin became something that is not good for me or others, and God was revealed as a God of great compassion who is simply trying to help me live the most fulfilling life possible; sin gets in the way of that. Instead of leaving confession feeling like a terrible sinner and hoping to do better next time and to keep "the rules," I left deeper in love with the God of love—the God who *is* love.

Confession is a meditative act that requires embodiment. We take our bodies to confession in order to fulfill the impulse behind confession; by going to confess we show that we have left what we're confessing behind. With our bodies we repent and literally turn from our old way of life. Jesus' parable in the Gospel of Luke verses 18:9-14 illustrates this well for us. There are two confessors: the Pharisee and the tax collector are seen at the temple praying. Both go to pray but only one makes confession—embodying his prayer by his posture and by beating his breast, which symbolized his internal humility. The other prays "about himself" (or as some texts have it, "to himself"). Only the tax collector leaves the temple justified.

Walking the Camino reminded me daily that I cannot live apart from being connected to my Creator and Redeemer—like the plump grapes on the vine that cannot survive apart from connection to the vine. That kind of connection is of the deepest intimacy—knowing God and being known by God. I wanted to settle for nothing less.

CONFUSED WESTERN SPIRITUALITY

Intimacy with God is possible when we believe in the reality of the divine indwelling as expressed through Scripture:

- I will ask the One who sent me to give you another Paraclete, another Helper to be with you always. (John 14:16)

- Aren't you aware that you are the temple of God, and that the Spirit of God dwells in you? (1 Corinthians 3:16)

- God is the One who firmly establishes us along with you in Christ; it is God who anointed us and sealed us, putting the Spirit in our hearts as our bond and guarantee. (2 Corinthians 1:21-22)

- God made us for this very purpose and gave us the pledge of the Spirit to safeguard our future. (2 Corinthians 5:5)

According to these and other references, God dwells within us. At Christian baptism, we receive a special grace and faith to grow in response to the presence of God. Contemplative prayer provides a way to grow in awareness of the Presence. Growing in awareness allows us to respond more readily to God. As we progress in the Christian journey, we find ourselves experiencing a divine dance of moving with the rhythm of the Spirit. As the dance develops in intimacy, union is possible. In union, we are most free from our self-consciousness and are in tune with the consciousness of God. In God we live, move and have our being. God's thoughts become our thoughts. God's ways become our ways. God initiates and we respond. God leads the dance; we follow in step. Like the most eloquent waltz or most enchanting salsa, we are mystified in the embrace of our Lover. The doctrine of the divine indwelling affirms God's immanence (the pervading presence of God within the created world), yet many of us live as if God is only transcendent (above, beyond and independent of the created world). The two attributes of God are important for us to understand so that we can grow in relationship with God.

Richard Hauser, S.J., in his book *Moving in the Spirit: Becoming a Contemplative in Action,* drives this point home in his reflection on Pelagius and the Western model of spirituality. Today there is great debate over Pelagius's teaching, but the point Hauser tries to make remains valid: many misunderstand grace and the immanent presence of God because we embrace a position that makes grace unnecessary and live out of touch with the immanent Presence.

Pelagius was recognized as a respected monk before his ideas surfaced. A teacher in Rome, he was thought to have originally been from Britain. Hauser simplifies the complicated history surrounding Pelagius's ideas by pointing to a debate that occurred between Pelagius and Augustine of Hippo—one of the most influential early church fathers. The controversy centered chiefly on original sin and the role of grace. Pelagius failed to understand humanity's nature and weakness as portrayed by various passages of Scripture.

A common reading of the Pelagian theory suggests that humanity is able to perform some good deeds apart from the grace of Christ. Jesus was important to the Pelagians not because of the indwelling grace released through his life, death and resurrection, but because he provided the example for humanity to follow. The early church countered this idea by affirming that Christ saves humanity through the indwelling Spirit and apart from human actions, work or the degree to which we can imitate Christ's example. The Pelagian theory is that we can do the will of God and attain goodness, virtue and holiness apart from the grace of God, entirely by our will. This theology amounted to the Western model of spirituality that suggests that the self exists outside of God—self initiates and God rewards. The measure of grace received is dependent on good behavior.[9]

Augustine led the movement to denounce this teaching[10] and correct it with a scriptural model of spirituality. The scriptural model is self-in-God—God initiates and we respond. Grace (or love) is experienced within this union of self-in-God. In response to the Pelagians, the church insisted that the movement in our hearts toward good action flows from our response to the grace of God, not on our own initiative. For fifteen hundred years Christians have affirmed that the desire for good and the power to carry it out flow from the grace of Christ.[11]

Orthodox Christian teaching reiterates that we, in our brokenness, are unable to fully do God's will. We *are* affected by original sin, contrary to Pelagianism. And Augustine and others were determined to preserve this truth.

Hauser describes these principles in figure 1.

WESTERN (PELAGIAN) MODEL:
SELF-OUTSIDE-GOD

SCRIPTURAL MODEL:
SELF-IN-GOD

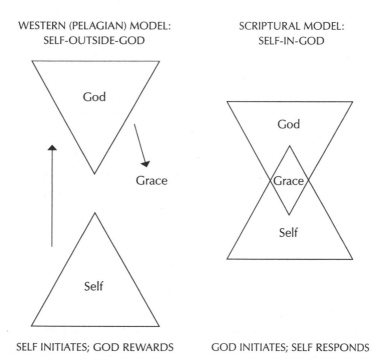

SELF INITIATES; GOD REWARDS

GOD INITIATES; SELF RESPONDS

Figure 1. Western Christian spirituality and biblical Christian spirituality

Illustrated on the left side of the diagram is the "Western Model of Spirituality." God and self are depicted apart from one another. Grace is understood as something outside of ourselves and therefore separated from the origin of our good action. Grace is something that God rewards us with for the good we do on our own initiative. Our good actions are understood to originate from self. The good in our lives flows apart from and independent of grace, while grace increases or decreases based on our behavior. Relationship with God centers on punishment and reward.

In the "Scriptural Model of Spirituality" diagram, we see the indwelling of God depicted. The intersecting triangles symbolize the presence of the Spirit as the origin for inner movements toward good. As we grow in union, we can imagine the intersection of triangles increasing—this signifies our growing posture of surrender and the increase of Christ's life freely flowing through us.[12]

Intimacy is possible when I trust myself to the One within whom I live and move and have my being (Acts 17:28). God revealed the extent of this union through the annunciation, by incarnating God's self in the world through Mary. Can the imagery be any clearer? The God of the universe is not somewhere out there, distant and separate from humanity. God entered into the very womb of Mary, which illustrates God's presence within all humanity. God initiates: God told Mary that though she was a virgin, she would conceive a son (Luke 1:31). God inhabited Mary's womb. Mary responded to the grace given her and was receptive to the will of God: "Let it be done to me according to Your word" (Luke 1:38). God initiates; self responds. God has not ceased to initiate with humanity. God has made God's home within me and you, but it is up to us to awaken to the Presence.

Reflecting on the season of Advent, Carla Mae Streeter in her book *Seasons of the Soul: An Intimate God in Liturgical Time* makes this point eloquently:

Mary is me. She is you, and you, and you. Mary is that humanness that is asked to bring forth God. . . . The message of God united with humanness in a woman's womb is the message that for me, too, locked in the darkness of faith's womb in this life, this Holy One is still taking on humanness: *mine.* Mary is a mirror. In her we find our own original face as God-bearer.[13]

Intimacy is possible when we recognize the immanent as well as the transcendent presence of God and join with the Presence in the creative process of life. Through an intimate exchange, abundant life unfolds. This is what Jesus tried to communicate in his promises of fullness of life, life eternal and the abundant life. Intimacy evokes abandonment to the object of love. Bathed in trust, we can abandon our self to the One who made us. And the Christian understanding of Christ living in us, the hope of glory, is made possible. Through this intimate exchange we are conformed to God's likeness.

7

UNION

Day THIRTY-THREE ON THE CAMINO, when Chris and I walked hand in hand into the early morning city of Santiago, we could scarcely believe we had really arrived. As we turned the corner, El Catedral de Santiago jutted up before our eyes. Its weathered, westward gates gave us a tired, overextended welcome. As we drew nearer, the massive structure looked down on us as it had countless pilgrims through the centuries. We were the only pilgrims in the plaza at that hour—just Chris, me and the ancient church welcoming us. We marked the moment with a warm embrace and took our personal thoughts to silence. We had arrived. We had made a sacred passage. Our presence would be announced in the afternoon pilgrims' mass—"Two pilgrims from Nebraska made it to Santiago by foot!"

My journal entry that day captures the arrival:

It's hard to get my mind and emotions around the moment. We really did it! We made it to Santiago on foot as we hoped and prayed and cried we would. . . . In addition to the very concrete destination of the cathedral, El Camino de Santiago leads to an internal place. The way is transforming for the body, mind and soul. And the internal destination is a place of peace—a peace that is found by the way in which we journeyed—open, abandoned, dependent, broken, stripped, humbled, receptive, loved.[1]

Lee Hoinacki is so right. "The Camino is not a path leading to Santiago, but a way to reach Christ—if one can learn how to walk on it."[2] We made it to Santiago, but in a way our sojourn had just begun.

During pilgrimage, Chris and I had reflected on various aspects of our lives—our marriage, vocation, community and friends who feel like family scattered all over the world (some of them still living in poverty). All the pieces of our lives were laid out before us, and upon reaching Santiago it seemed they had been brought back together in a more proper way through our conversations, reflections and prayer. The parts had become a whole and there was a sense of union to what had been fragmented. Parts of me that had been in hiding were coming into focus and I was offering those parts of myself to Chris with courage and honesty, evaluating how those parts would be offered anew to my normal, actively engaged life. False ways in which I had previously responded and reacted to my husband, my community and the world were being revealed. The interpersonal self was giving way to the institutional self, bringing the fragmented parts of my life into a whole. The inter-individual self seemed within reach.

The spiritual journey offers a similar experience of union—fragmented parts of our self becoming whole. Classic Christian spirituality describes the Christian sojourn in terms of three stages: the purgative way, the illuminative way and the unitive way. The purgative way is where we begin. As we grow closer to God we move into the illuminative way. And at a point of responding to God in love and living primarily out of that love, one is said to be in the unitive way. The Fathers and Mothers of the church teach that at each stage there are different prayer practices that aid our spiritual growth. Richard Hauser describes this in an outline called "The Christian Spiritual Path" (see table 1).[3]

As you look at the table you'll notice three columns: "Stages of the Journey," "Focus of Daily Living" and "Quality of Prayer." Each stage in the spiritual journey corresponds with a particular focus that characterizes it ("Focus of Daily Living") and a particular type of prayer ("Quality of Prayer") that usually marks that stage in the journey.

The spiritual journey is a multilayered process where we often vacillate between stages (especially before we reach the unitive

Table 1. The Christian Spiritual Path

Stages of the Journey	Focus of Daily Living	Quality of Prayer
Unawakened Self	Law & Commandments	Vocal
	(Relationship to Christ by fidelity to obligations)	
	AWAKENING OF THE SELF TO THE SPIRIT (Relationship to Christ by fidelity to the Spirit)	
Purgative Way	Imitation of Christ: Patterns of action Continuing Conversion: Temptations Fluctuations of heart Fluctuations of action	Talking to the Lord Mind active Meditation
Illuminative Way	Imitation of Christ: Quality of heart Continuing Conversion: Temptations Fluctuations of heart *No* fluctuation of action	Being with the Lord Mind attentive: I-Thou Beginning contemplations
Unitive Way	Imitation of Christ: Zeal for service Continuing Conversion: Temptations *No* fluctuation of heart *No* fluctuation of action	Being one in the Lord Mind absorbed in the Lord Advanced contemplation

way). All of the prayer practices are valuable at each stage, but the emphasis for growth lies in the "Quality of Prayer" column. In other words, the prayer practices ("Talking to the Lord," "Being with the Lord," "Being one in the Lord") indicated at each stage are best, or are naturally supported, by the quality of prayer ("Mind active," "Mind attentive," "Mind absorbed in the Lord") indicated. But each stage is not limited to this type of prayer. As one progresses in the journey, one moves through awakening to purgation, illumination and union. Each stage aids the continual conversion process we experience as we grow in relationship with God. Some compare these classic Christian-spirituality descriptive stages with the more contemporary terms "woundedness," "recovery" and "wellness."[4] However you understand the stages, the end result is growing in increasing wholeness, or union.

Contemplative prayer usually marks the unitive way. But there is no foolproof prescription for reaching the unitive way and no cookie-cutter practice that indicates one has reached it. The all-pervasive quality of love in one's life is the only probable indication that one is living in a state of union with God.

Contemplation as mentioned in this chart is understood as the state of prayer or awareness. Contemplation in this sense is a gift, and as such it is not necessarily imparted to everyone. We must not confuse contemplation with contemplative prayer. We can practice contemplative prayer or acts of contemplation by our will; but we cannot will the contemplative state of union with God—it is a grace and a gift. The marks of the unitive way are most notably peace, freedom from compulsions and freedom from major agitation. In addition, the individual's mind and heart are almost continuously fixed on God. Reaching the unitive way involves a dreadful experience of purgation and abandonment (described by John of the Cross as a "dark night" of darkness and death) which has the effect of freeing one from the false self. This freedom results in personal strength, power, energy and selfless giving of the purest, freest kind.[5]

The point of axis for the state of union is love. When living in the unitive way, we are free to receive and give love. Our motivations are rooted in love rather than in ego-centered compulsions or "programs for happiness." The true self is alive and active.

GETTING READY TO RETURN: FROM ME TO EVERYONE

In the memoir *Eat, Pray, Love,* Elizabeth Gilbert realizes at the end of her year-long journey in search of her self that "when you set out in the world to help yourself, you inevitably end up helping everyone."[6] When Gilbert reached her final destination in her journey through India, Italy and Indonesia she met a little Balinese girl whose name, Tutti, means "everybody" in Italian. Having uncovered her hidden self, Gilbert was more authentically attentive and responsive to a little girl and her family in need. From a place of freedom and love, Gilbert responded to the needs of this family with courage and generosity. She even compelled others to get involved in the liberation of the family. Gilbert realized that embracing her deepest self allows for an encounter with God, and that encounter connects us with everyone. When we are connected to God we cannot remain isolated and indifferent to the needs of others. The needs of the world call to the truest part of us that was created to respond in our unique way with courage and creativity.

The difference at the point of union is how we respond to those needs. Rather than responding from a place of false attachments and compulsions—the need for power and control, affection and esteem, or security and survival—we respond from a place of freedom from those attachments; a place of pure, undefiled love. We love with no expectation of return.

I struggled a lot at the beginning of sabbatical, thinking that taking all of that time for me was selfish. But I came to understand, like Gilbert, that sacred time of solitude and rest, whether it be a weekly sabbath or once a year or every seventh year or so, is really

for everybody. In fact we owe it to the world to create time and
space for dismantling our illusions. Otherwise we may be guilty of
committing acts of violence. As Thomas Merton wrote,

> To allow oneself to be carried away by a multitude of con-
> flicting concerns, to surrender oneself to too many demands,
> to commit oneself to too many projects, to want to help ev-
> eryone in everything is to succumb to violence. More than
> that, it is cooperation in violence. It destroys one's own ca-
> pacity for peace. It destroys the fruitfulness of one's own
> work, because it kills the root of inner wisdom which makes
> the work fruitful.[7]

Living into our true self, being free of our ego and rooted in love
allows for true acts of peace and justice. Without attention to our
internal motivations and attachments, we are at risk of imposing
our will on the world—deceived into thinking we are doing a virtuous thing—only to find out we need forgiveness for our action
(the sin of omission more often than that of commission). The ways
we interact with the world can be connected so deeply to our false
self that we cause more harm than good. In our misapprehension
we do not realize that what we are doing may actually be reaping
destruction cloaked in virtue. The greater our leadership and influence, the greater the potential domination and devastation. How
else can we explain nations at war with one another, global exploi-
tation of the poor, destruction to our planet?

During sabbatical, I was learning how necessary contemplative
spirituality is to dismantling my illusions and uncovering my true
self. All the months of distress and agony were transforming me.
And at moments the anguish, disorientation and darkness sub-
sided, to hint at peaceful union ahead.

In the fall of our sabbatical, Chris and I spent Thanksgiving
with our friend Amey Victoria and her family in rural Rocky
Mount, Virginia. What a delight to be strangers welcomed in and

warmly embraced around the family feasting table. The drive out was breathtaking, winding through autumn wooded roads filled with deer, the green, red, yellow and orange leaves falling and blowing in the wind. The season was changing. The season of my soul was changing too; love was taking root.

Sabbatical was a sacred time for me. A season of time and space opened before me, inviting me to deeper solitude, silence and stillness. Weekly sabbath and regular private retreats offer the same invitation. All throughout sabbatical my thoughts returned to a familiar poem. I found myself identifying with the psalmist's expression of a similar experience:

> The LORD is my shepherd, I shall not be in want.
>   He makes lie down in green pastures,
> he leads me beside quiet waters,
>   he restores my soul. . . .
> Though I walk
>   through the valley of the shadow of death,
> I will fear no evil,
>   for you are with me;
> your rod and your staff,
>   they comfort me.
>
> You prepare a table before me
>   in the presence of my enemies. . . .
>   My cup overflows.
> Surely goodness and love will follow me
>   all the days of my life,
> and I will dwell in the house of the LORD
>   forever. (Psalm 23 NIV)

Certainly the Lord was and is my Shepherd. Like a good shepherd with her not-so-intelligent sheep, God knew my need before I did. The essence of the spiritual journey is so evident in this psalm. The "Shepherd" makes me lie down, but also leads me; restores my soul even as I walk through the valley of death; prepares a table for me and sets me on a good and merciful path; makes a home for me while never neglecting to care for me.

God made me lie down in green pastures. Through God's generous and gracious provision, I was able to experience a pilgrimage of a lifetime. For a month in time I was transported from the trenches of an active life of pursuing and building communities of justice, compassion and peace, to the rolling, green hills of the Spanish countryside where wildflowers grew along the roadside and vineyards were laid out before me in all their splendor. The expanse of the blue sky was my canopy and the rich soil my carpet. I would wake with the sunrise and be greeted by the natural wonders of the earth every moment of the day.

I remember one day in particular when Chris and I made a difficult climb over an arid hillside with massive boulders and rocks underfoot. With every step my feet and ankles burned with pain; the Scripture about how God makes our path straight made so much sense to me. My body needed a straight path. Finally, after a couple of hours of ascending this hill we reached the top. And as we descended, a massive expanse of green, plush grass greeted us. The way was made straight, and the green pastures were literally provided for us. I broke down in tears as I received this most precious gift to my body and soul.

God led me beside still waters. For five months I was able to bring my active life to a halt and enter the stillness of the second part of my sabbatical at Duke. Five months of utter stillness, the waters of the ocean and that much-needed rainstorm.

God restored my soul. During those months of rest, God tended and restored my soul and sense of self.

God led me through darkness. I had never experienced such intense feelings of abandonment by God. The darkness I endured was like nothing I had ever known. As my life and sense of self seemed to be crumbling, God was with me. Jesus kept me. God led the way through that most disturbing season.

God prepared a table for me. And all the while as I submitted to the transformative work of God—like the caterpillar in her cocoon—God was preparing a place for me to return to, a table spread out for me to engage in a more life-giving way.

Truly my cup overflows. As I write this, my "cup" overflows—this "feeler" is spilling out tears in wonder at what God has done for her. I could not have made this journey alone. How can I not love the One who has done all of this for me?

During the last week or so of sabbatical, I grieved to say goodbye to that sweet season. I knew I would miss the long mornings—waking only when my body and mind decided to awake, lingering in prayer, reading and reflecting—free from nearly all responsibilities and obligations. I knew I would miss the quantity of relaxed, unscheduled, unhurried time by myself and with Chris and new friends. I would miss the sacred long walks and long soaks in the hot tub. I would miss the gift of Durham and Duke Divinity School and the short distance from the seaside. But I realized that there is a time for everything—a time to rest and a time to engage. A time for solitude and a time for embrace. And I realized that there was something I missed that could not be found in the same way in North Carolina. I missed the community of Word Made Flesh.

COMMUNITY AND CREATIVE ABSENCE

Jara, a friend and coworker at Word Made Flesh, gave us a handmade bowl as we were preparing to leave for sabbatical. "It isn't until we are empty—like this bowl," she wrote, "that we can fully embrace solitude and welcome each other more intimately in our lives." The months of sabbath rest truly had been a time of self-emptying—emptying the false parts of self that hindered my true self from emerging. Greater intimacy was now possible. For several months that year I was separated from my people—making room for solitude between us. I was challenged in new ways to trust that this grand solitude of sabbatical could truly be for my people as well as for me.

Nouwen explains this paradox of solitude and relationship:

> In solitude we come to know our fellow human beings not as partners who satisfy our deepest needs, but as brothers and sisters with whom we are called to give visibility to God's all-embracing love. In solitude we discover that family or community is not some common ideology but a response to a common call. In solitude we indeed experience that community is not made but given. . . .
>
> Whenever we enter into solitude, we witness to a love that transcends our interpersonal communications and proclaims that we love each other because we have been loved first (1 Jn 4:19). Solitude keeps us in touch with the sustaining love from which we draw strength. It sets us free from the compulsions of fear and anger and allows us to be in the midst of an anxious and violent world as a sign of hope and a source of courage.[8]

Emerging from a creative absence from my community, I realized how much I wanted to be with them. I wanted to reconnect with my brothers and sisters. I wanted to return to them. My love for them had grown. I had never been more grateful for my community. I knew that I would be able to best express my deepest self in their company, rather than in perpetual isolation. Instead of being defined by my relationships, I wanted to *be in* relationship (interpersonal vs. inter-individual). It's an incredible gift to be part of a community that is a sign of hope and courage in a despairing, violent world. Chris and I are members of a community of incredible children, women and men who bring us life, and within their company God's all-embracing love is brought into focus. I looked forward to being connected with them again—this time in a freer, truer sense, and hopefully from a place rooted deeper in 1 .c. I looked forward also to being reconnected with Chris in our active life together. The transformation I had experienced was transforming our marriage also. Letting our transformed sense of self and marriage take flight was a longing to be realized.

Sabbatical was a necessary time of detaching, self-emptying, and becoming naked and vulnerable in deeper ways; and returning became time to reattach and engage community in new ways. By reengaging I would know whether or not solitude had made an empty, sacred space within me in which I could welcome all people. As Nouwen suggests, "There is a powerful connection between our emptiness and our ability to welcome."[9]

That December, after closing the chapter on a season at Duke, Chris and I drove our little, black Toyota Yaris all the way from Durham, North Carolina, to Omaha, Nebraska. As we entered Omaha and turned onto North Thirty-Third Street we started to approach our home. To our surprise, at the corner we spotted a yellow arrow! They were posted all the way down the road, leading to the front door of our apartment. Our friends in community had heard the stories of the arrows on the Camino and after a long separation welcomed us with these markers to reassure us that we had found our way.

A VOICE CALLING

When we are rooted in love—in union with God—simple, congruent communities made up of healthy relationships are formed, and service rather than domination is possible. True service is the expression of our vocation, our response to love.

The English word "vocation" is derived from the Latin *vocare*, "to call" and *vox*, "voice." The meaning centers on a "voice calling." John Neafsey, a clinical psychologist and senior lecturer in the department of theology at Loyola University Chicago, says that "vocation is not only about 'me' and my personal fulfillment, but about 'us' and the common good." He goes on to explain that "authentic vocational discernment, therefore, seeks a proper balance between inward listening *to* our heart and outward, socially engaged listening *with* our heart to the realities of the world in which we live. These come together in our heart's response to the needs and sufferings of the world."[10]

Living in a place of union opens us to our true voice, our vocation. Service is refined and redefined. We live from the truth of who we are, rather than our false-self "programs for happiness." When we live in this way, we respond to the plea of Christ in his crucifixion. For many years, I understood the crucifixion mostly as an indictment against my ugliness, unworthiness and sinfulness. This perception stands in stark contrast to the message of Christ's life. John Main explains it this way:

> The crucifixion is the divine plea to each of us to understand the meaning and wonder of our creation, the dignity which love bestows. . . . [I]n knowing this we open our hearts to the reality of our personal destiny, far beyond the narrow confines of the ego. The astonishing core of the Christian revelation is that the destiny of each person is full union with God, "to share in the very being of God," as St. Peter puts it. . . .
>
> Perhaps the greatest problem afflicting our society is that so many people feel that they are not fully alive. They suffer the sense that they are not fully authentic as human beings. A major reason for this is that there are so many living their life second-hand without a real openness to the uniqueness of the gift given to them: their own life.
>
> So many lives are lived by responding to other people's goals for us. . . . Christian revelation says that each of us is summoned to respond directly to the fullness of our own life in the mystery of God.[11]

On the cross, Christ experienced the totality of solitude, silence and stillness—the feeling of having no followers, no sympathizers, no companions, no God. But his return from solitude on the third day changed everything, ushering in the new creation and the new vocation of his people. Withdrawing at times from our virtuous, active life offers us the opportunity to identify with Christ in his absolute abandonment. And from that kind of encounter with the Divine, our action is purified, our destiny is unleashed, we grow in intimacy and we are more likely to experience union.

It is difficult to hear the voice of God calling us to fullness of life amidst the dissonance of other voices that filter through our "programs for happiness." But regular periods of solitude, silence and stillness provide a way to dismantle the dissonance. Contemplative practices provide a way to cut through the static and noise that lead us away from the voice of God. Slowly, slowly in the company of a patient God and supportive community we can find the ability to respond to "the fullness of our own life in the mystery of God." Throughout our lifetimes our vocations will develop and evolve as we grow and mature. Our response to the fullness of our lives in the mystery of God will look a particular way at each stage in our lives. All along the journey we do the best we can at the time to live and respond with integrity and truth. As time goes on, with ever-deepening awareness and freedom, our truest selves are set free.

When our sabbatical came to a close and Chris and I reentered an active life of service, some subtle and some not-so-subtle changes unfolded. I had emerged from my cocoon and it was time to test my wings. Awakened to the divine feminine, I had uncovered courage to assert myself in new ways. With greater self-awareness, I was compelled to engage the world in a way that would be true to these realized parts of myself. I was determined to assert myself appropriately in all of my relationships and creative work—in a way that would allow me to be fully present and not tempted to hide. Being free from the "program of happiness" for affection and esteem, I asserted myself at the risk of being misunderstood or rejected.

A part of the change my true self demanded of me was expressed in becoming Catholic. Also, in Word Made Flesh I gained confidence to imagine a new organizational position that would best serve the community while allowing me to live into my potential; honoring my deepest self *and* serving others was possible. The two are not mutually exclusive. Contrary to the distorted message I received as a woman, the two are inherently connected. Whereas I had formerly hidden myself (in a manner of "self-sacrifice") and allowed my potential and influence to be dictated by relationships or circumstances (in a manner of feminine subordination) through the flow from my encounters of union these fragmented parts were becoming whole. Rooted in love, my true self was free to be expressed in all areas of life. My vocation continued to evolve into ever-widening layers of truth from which my deep gladness could connect with the world's deep hunger.[12]

Reflecting on the changes in me, Chris, my marriage and my community, I have thought often about the homily at our wedding. Dr. Samuel Kamaleson, our dear friend, mentor and officiate, reflected on 1 Corinthians 6:19-20: "You are not your own. You have been bought with a price." He simply but soberly charged us to remember that we belong to God, one another and the world. These commitments keep us anchored and allow for periodic refinement of how we relate to God, each other and the world—depending on where we're at in our personal pilgrimage.

Each of our lives does not look like anyone else's. The uniqueness of our life created in the image of God is meant to shine. Our very own life is a gift to be given. We each have a unique vocation, and it is brought into community with others. Isn't this the diversity we see in the Gospels? Some left prestigious work to follow Jesus. Others, after being touched by Christ, returned to a rather "normal" life in society. There are many stories of Jesus telling some to leave everything and follow him, and others he told to return to their village. The call or vocation looked different for each one. And it looks different for each of us. The invitation is to know God and be known by God—authentic life and relationship. In that place of intimacy we are more inclined toward union and therefore freer to be who God created us to be.

The beauty of our lives is our participation in the paschal mystery of Christ again and again. With each new passage of death we receive new revelations of love. We continue in this cyclical pilgrimage until that final day when we will make our last passage from death to life and find ourselves in eternal, constant union with the One whom we have longed for since we took our first breath.

CONCLUSION

From Compulsion to Freedom

FOR MUCH OF OUR LIVES we are bound by the "emotional junk of a lifetime." I have had to come to terms with my own false-self "programs for happiness." I had previously lived in a mode of reaction like Parker Palmer describes so well (see chapter five).[1] Bound by the interpersonal stage of development, I was driven by a need to be needed and I reacted accordingly. I was not always serving from a "free and independent heart." I did not have a good sense of my deepest self but rather was driven by who I thought I was expected to be by family, friends and the religious community. Patriarchal paradigms reinforced this posture of captivity. In some ways, I was letting others define me instead of the One who created me.

Our emotional wounds of a lifetime need healing. During a visit to St. Benedict's Monastery in Snowmass, Colorado, I was told by Father Micah that prayer is healing. It doesn't always feel good. In the healing of a physical wound, as the body rejuvenates there is itching and pain. Likewise, as we grow and heal we journey through seven movements: awakening, longing, darkness, death, transformation, intimacy and union. Our healing and growth often come through pain and suffering.

But in the unitive way, there is only one descriptor—love. Love defines. Love motivates. Love responds instead of reacts. Contemplative practices provide the space to move from compulsion to freedom. Contemplative prayer is a way in which we connect to love and absorb the truth of our belovedness and our unique destiny. Being grounded in the truth of who we are sets us free to live authentically, responding with generosity and creativity to the needs before us and, in turn, receiving gifts offered. As we live in the limitlessness of God's Spirit, we experience freedom like the apostle Paul wrote about: "Now the Lord is the Spirit; and where the Spirit of the Lord is, there is freedom" (2 Corinthians 3:17). Contemplative prayer is a way to grow in union because through this prayer the love and freedom of God become more corporeal to us.

Centering prayer (sometimes called "pure prayer" or "prayer of heartfulness") is a simple prayer that supports the spiritual journey. It is adapted from a prayer practice that was historically confined to monasteries and convents, dating back to the Desert Mothers and Fathers of the third century. In the 1960s and 70s, a surge conspired to make this prayer available to laypeople. Monks like Thomas Merton, Basil Pennington, Thomas Keating and John Main were monumental contributors to this movement. Because of the overwhelming response of individuals, Keating established a worldwide community of contemplatives called Contemplative Outreach. Different leaders teach the prayer slightly differently, but the principles are the same.

Silence is God's first language, according to mystics. And in centering prayer, silence is the language of communication. For twenty to thirty minutes, two times a day (though this time can be shortened in the beginning when one is getting used to it), we sit in silence with God and consent to God's presence and action within us. The use of a sacred word symbolizes our intention to consent to the presence and action. When first beginning the practice, we wait in silence to receive our sacred word. This can be any word or short phrase that symbolizes our relationship with God. It could be our favorite word for referencing God or a characteristic of God, like love, peace, joy and so on. Over time, the sacred word can change, but it is best to keep the word consistent so as not to be distracted by the changing of the word. Certainly it is discouraged to change the word *during* a prayer period. And if one wants to change their word over the course of time, it is recommended to discuss the change with one's spiritual director.

Centering prayer is a practice that is quite difficult for people of Western culture who overemphasize connecting to God through the faculties (reason, imagination, memory, feelings and will). This prayer is not unreasonable for Christians; it is beyond reason. This is a different way of connecting our whole self to God. It teaches us awareness, presence, embodiment, trust, surrender, faith and hope. This prayer is not intended to usurp other prayers or sacred practices but to be used in addition to them. Throughout the entire prayer period, thoughts that flood our minds give way to our sacred word, which represents our intention to give God our undivided attention. In some ways it might be helpful to think of this "prayer" as a discipline more than prayer as we commonly understand it—conversation in words, feelings of consolation and the like. Centering prayer disciplines our souls to be aware of and attentive to God in our active life. The fruit of this prayer is seen in our active life, and so we should not concern ourselves with an experience during prayer or with seeking after consolations during the prayer. We abandon everything—all desires, anxieties, expectations and energies—as a way of being present to the Presence.

Our office community makes time in the middle of our work day at 3:00 p.m. to come to God together in this silent prayer. During frenetic activity, many of us stop to find rest in God. In this way we remember that we are finite and only God is infinite, and we affirm our dependence on God. We cultivate an awareness and attentiveness to the presence of God to become more naturally aware of God's presence in all of our activity. This prayer time connects and roots us to the Spirit who dwells within us, who in turn connects us with our entire community spread out across the globe. It is a way of "remaining in Jesus" (vine and branches, John 15) that we might bear lasting fruit. By honoring this rhythm of action and contemplation we nurture intimacy with God and bear lasting fruit in our active lives. As Thomas Merton explained, our active lives are "leavened by peace, order and clarity."[2] As we spend time with God in contemplative prayer we experience greater freedom from our false-self motivations and compulsions and receive fullness of life. Contemplative prayer brings into focus our gifts and therefore we know more clearly and more freely where to focus our energies. This is the dance of contemplation and action.

The union of action and contemplation brings freedom and joy—even in the midst of some of the greatest poverty and suffering of our time. By abandoning ourselves regularly to God through prayer in the form of solitude, silence and stillness, we experience more freedom *from* compulsions and heavy-laden expectations and more liberty *in* our true self with all of our unique gifts to offer the world. Bringing balance to action and contemplation in our lives allows for the greatest impact in our world. And the love of God compels us to not lose heart in the journey.

Awakening, longing, darkness, death, transformation, intimacy and union. The spiritual journey is an intense sojourn. Where are you in the pilgrimage? Who do you long to be? Is your life fragmented or are you experiencing the peace of union?

Picture yourself at the end of your long journey:

Warming yourself at the fireplace, you watch the flames dance softly across the wall. Your pilgrimage has come to an end. You have traveled to the outer limits of your being and returned home full of a sense of worth, and a profound understanding of who you are.

You turn and in the doorway stands a young pilgrim. She

is so young, her eyes so bright. There is a beauty about her, an eagerness to be on her way. You wonder if this was what you were like so long ago when, staff in hand, you first stepped out on the road.

"What can you tell me about the journey?" she asks. What dare you tell her?

"You will be met by demons and angels. You will have nights of crystal clarity and dark days of doubt. You will lose your way so many times you can't keep count. But over and over, you will stumble upon yourself, and in the end grow to love who you are."[3]

As we grow to love who we are, we grow in capacity to love God and one another. The spiritual journey is as much about loving our self as it is about loving our neighbor. "Love your neighbor as yourself" (Matthew 22:39). If we are not giving proper care and attention to our deepest self, we are at the least encumbered in our love of others and at the most committing acts of violence in the name of love. We owe it to the world to submit to a spiritual journey that makes us receptive to the dismantling of our illusions and self-deceit. We can be either our worst enemy or our dearest friend. For the love of God, let us choose the latter. For in befriending our self, we find the One who calls us and even our enemy "Beloved." From this centered place of union we can hope to bear witness to redemptive love and to live as cocreators with God.

Buen camino,
Phileena

ACKNOWLEDGMENTS

THE EVENING I RECEIVED the final edits for this book, I was on my way out the door to attend one of my favorite yoga classes. As I breezed through the finished pages of what had become my first book, I felt a surge of emotion within me. I hurriedly embraced the feeling of accomplishment and finishing well, and made my way to class. The ninety-minute practice of the evening focused on back bends—a series of postures I wasn't very familiar with. At the end of the session, when it was time for *savasana* (corpse pose, in which we lay flat on our backs for several minutes to complete our practice), I was surprised to find tears quietly streaming out of my eyes, into my ears and falling softly on the mat. After we came to a seated position to acknowledge the effort of one another and to bring closure, my yoga instructor, Jed, kindly asked, "Are you okay?" That evening it was only Jed, his wife, Sarah, and me in class, so it felt intimate and safe. I asked, "Is it common to experience these kinds of emotions during yoga?" And they both proceeded to explain that it *is* common, especially after a session of back bends.

What I learned in those moments was the beauty of embodiment and how the varied layers of our lives come together. In class as I practiced the postures of back bends, I was opening my heart center—the place of love, compassion and vulnerability. And the exposure of the bodily heart center has the potential to open up some of the most vulnerable expressions of who we are. Normally the average person tends toward hiding and protecting his or her most vulnerable space—symbolized in the front body and heart center. But in class that night, I was opening that body space and also the intangible space of my vulnerable soul.

Just before class, as I reviewed the page proofs, I was experiencing the culmination of a journey I had been on for years. Through my book, my "heart center"—the seat of some of my most vulnerable places—was being exposed, soon for literally the world to see. My body and soul harmonized through the embodiment of courageous and vulnerable yoga postures. The result was emotional release of peace, love, joy and gratitude.

My teachers explained that in the tradition of yoga they practice, the front side of the body is the "individual body." The backside of the body is the "universal body." One supports the other. And so in the moments of *savasana*, as I experienced the liberation of exposing my heart center, I also became overwhelmed with gratitude for the support that has enabled me to put myself out there in the world through the expression of *Pilgrimage of a Soul*.

Immediately my thoughts turned to specific mentors who have nurtured, supported and believed in me at unique stages of my life: to my parents, Phil and Sandy Bacon; to Patrick and Victoria Samuel; and to Michael and Laura Alley. There are so many others who have accompanied me in my journey along the way—who were provided at just the right time, in just the perfect way. For each of you I am deeply grateful. A few I am compelled to mention: Eva Joyce Cunningham (my late "Mammaw"), Dr. Samuel and Adela Kamaleson, Fr. Bert Thelan, Dr. Cathy Leslie, and Bob and Anne Ginn.

Beyond these guides, there are some friends who were particular companions in the actual writing of the book. There is a common proverb: "It takes a village to raise a child." Well, it took a small village to write *Pilgrimage of a Soul*. My heartfelt gratitude is warmly extended to you who accompanied me and supported me with your readings and constructive feedback: Adriana Dakimow-icz Forcatto, Amey Victoria Atkins, Bethel Lee, David Bayne, Sonya Gray, Stuart Erny and Twyla O'Callaghan. For your technical assistance I am so grateful: Hilary Wilken, Mandy Mowers and Rob O'Callaghan.

To every single person at InterVarsity Press who had a hand in bringing this book to its beautiful completion, my sincerest thanks. A special appreciation to Jeff Crosby, associate publisher of sales and marketing, for your particular enthusiasm for the book at its proposal; Cindy Kiple, art director, for going above and beyond in creativity for cover design; Rebecca Carhart, copyeditor; Ruth Curphey, Adrianna Wright and every member of the sales and marketing team who is supporting the work and making it accessible to the reader. And for being the first to read my feeble writing, for believing in me and my voice, and for teaching me how to be a better writer: thank you David Zimmerman, associate editor for IVP Books. It's been a delight to work with you.

Beauty inspires creative work, and so there are two artists I'd like to extend a special thanks to. India.Arie: you sing many of my heart songs, and in the early days of drafting this manuscript, your music gave me the inspiration I needed. Thank you. And Sarah Lance: your life is beauty and your art has the potential to lead the reader further than my words. Thank you for being a part of this.

Thank you also to my community at Word Made Flesh—to the board for believing in and supporting my voice; to my coworkers for graciously extending to me the time and space needed to devote to writing; and to those I like to affectionately refer to as the "Third Order" of Word Made Flesh—the many friends and family who support our mission with your prayer and financial support. And to all of the women, men and children who I've come to know on impoverished urban streets, in degrading brothels and other desperate dwellings—my indebted gratitude to you for sharing your vulnerable lives with me. In you I find courage to be human. Thank you for your forgiveness, grace, love and confidence. May this book and my life, in some way, honor you.

And to the one whom I love more than life itself—Chris Heuertz—my best friend and cherished husband. Your life inspires and teaches me. Thank you for always believing in me and for seeing more in me than I can usually see in myself. Thank you for affirming the importance of this book, and for your support and assistance all along the way. Thank you for making this journey with me—and not just the book. Your companionship, love and support all these years is unmatched.

NOTES

Introduction

[1]Thomas Keating is a modern Christian mystic. For more than fifty years he has given himself to the ancient Christian contemplative tradition. Through contemplative prayer he has excelled in the fruits and gifts of the Spirit. He is wise and holy, discerning and kind. His life bears witness to the presence of Christ living within him. He is rooted in the Presence. And from the heart and mind of Christ, Fr. Thomas responds to the world around him. Being anchored in the real, immanent and transcendent presence of God frees him to respond as Jesus would. Through his efforts and those of others like him, he has renewed the Christian contemplative tradition and made it accessible to monks, nuns and laypeople alike. His teaching illuminates the gospel and provides a road map for the spiritual journey.

[2]The true self is our most liberated, deepest self in contrast to the false self who lives from a place of bondage, woundedness and fear. I will expand on this concept throughout the book. For further reading on the true and false self consider the following books: David Benner, *The Gift of Being Yourself;* Albert Haase, *Coming Home to Your True Self;* M. Basil Pennington, *True Self/False Self;* Thomas Merton, *The New Man.*

[3]I owe this imagery in part to Henri Nouwen (with Philip Roderick, *Beloved: Henri Nouwen in Conversation* [Grand Rapids: Eerdmans, 2007], p. 23).

[4]Exodus 20:8-11: "Remember the Sabbath day and keep it holy! For six days you will labor and do all your work, but the seventh day is a Sabbath for YHWH. Do no work on that day, neither you nor your daughter nor your son, nor your workers—women or men—nor your animals, nor the foreigner who lives among you. For in the six days YHWH made the heavens and the earth and the sea and all that they hold, but rested on the seventh day; this is why YHWH has blessed the Sabbath day and made it sacred."

[5]There are many kinds of contemplative prayer practices, like *lectio divina,* labyrinth prayer, breath prayer, the Welcome Prayer and prayer of recollection. For a good overview of these or other contemplative prayer practices see *Spiritual Disciplines Handbook: Practices That Transform Us,* by Adele Ahlberg Calhoun (Downers Grove, Ill.: InterVarsity Press, 2005). I explain centering prayer in more detail in chapter seven.

[6]The paschal mystery refers to the suffering or passion, death, resurrection, and glorification or ascension of Jesus Christ. The center of the work that the Father God sent Jesus the Son to do on earth is the paschal mystery. The term *paschal* comes from a Hebrew word meaning "the passing over." The paschal mystery is Jesus' passing over from earthly life through his passion, death, resurrection and ascension to a new and glorified life with the Father.

[7]Thomas Keating, *The Human Condition: Contemplation and Transformation* (New York: Paulist, 1999), pp. 18-19.

[8]In the Torah, the seventh year is known as the sabbatical year. Exodus 23:10-11: "You may sow your crops and reap them for six years, but in the seventh year let it rest and lie untilled. In that year the land will provide food for the poor, and what they don't take will go to the wild animals. Do the same with your vineyards and olive groves."

Chapter 1: Awakening

[1]Austin Reparth, "Starting Out," in *Pilgrim Cards* (accessed June 10, 2009) <www.pilgrimcards.com/>.

[2]Esknath Easwaran, *To Love Is to Know Me* (Tomales, Calif.: Nilgiri Press, 1993), p. 87.

[3]This translation is gender-neutral though the pronoun used is "he."

[4]Thomas Keating, *The Paschal Mystery: A Journey into Redemption and Grace* (Butler, N.J.: Contemplative Outreach, 2007), p. 100.

[5]In this tradition pastors are generally referred to as ministers or preachers instead of pastors.

[6]Debi Pearl, *Created to Be His Help Meet* (Pleasantville, Tenn.: No Greater Joy, 2004), p. 23.

[7]Ibid., p. 25.

[8]Ibid., p. 29.

[9]Ibid., pp. 31-32.

[10]Ibid., p. 23.

[11]I owe this insight to my gifted spiritual director, Sr. Anne Pellegrino, O.S.M.

[12]Marianne Williamson, *A Return to Love: Reflections on the Principles of a*

Course in Miracles (New York: HarperCollins, 1992), pp. 190-91.

[13]Reinhold Niebuhr was a leading American Protestant theologian of the twentieth century. He is credited with writing the Serenity Prayer. Carol Lakey Hess is a practical theologian and author of *Caretakers of Our Common House: Women's Development in Communities of Faith*. In her book, Hess says that few theologians have influenced North American theology as significantly as Niebuhr. She says that his theological anthropology both looked to historical key thinkers and themes in the Protestant tradition and projected forward a highly influential thought for Christian theology. And she remarks that his thought has raised critical questions for women. Carol Lakey Hess, *Caretakers of Our Common House: Women's Development in Communities of Faith* (Nashville: Abingdon, 1997), p. 33.

[14]Reinhold Niebuhr, *The Nature and Destiny of Man, Vol. 1: Human Nature* (New York: Scribner's Sons, 1941), pp. 137-38.

[15]Hess, *Caretakers of Our Common House*, pp. 34-35.

[16]Kate Hurley, "Hey Little Girl," from her album *Sleeping When You Woke Me* (Worship Circle Records, 2006).

[17]Niebuhr, *Nature and Destiny of Man*, pp. 137-38.

[18]Thomas Keating, *The Human Condition: Contemplation and Transformation* (New York: Paulist, 1999), p. 30.

[19]Ibid.

[20]Thomas Merton, *The New Man* (New York: Noonday Press, 1961), pp. 67, 63.

[21]For more information visit <www.dmiisinstitute.com/>.

[22]Personal journal, April 1, 2007.

[23]Parker J. Palmer, *The Active Life: A Spirituality of Work, Creativity, and Caring* (San Francisco: Jossey-Bass, 1990), p. 17.

[24]There are many books written about the Desert Fathers and Mothers. A couple I recommend are *The Wisdom of the Desert* by Thomas Merton and *The Forgotten Desert Mothers* by Laura Swan.

[25]John Main, *Word Made Flesh* (New York: Continuum, 1998), pp. 7-9.

[26]Thomas Keating, *Open Mind, Open Heart: The Contemplative Dimension of the Gospel* (New York: Continuum, 1986), p. 68.

[27]Keating, *Paschal Mystery*, p. 65.

[28]Thomas Keating, *Intimacy with God* (New York: Crossroad, 1994), p. 45.

[29]Thomas Keating, *The Spiritual Journey* video series, produced by Contemplative Outreach (n.d.).

[30]Keating, *Human Condition*, p. 36.

[31]Ibid., p. 35.

[32]Thomas Keating, *The Better Part* (New York: Continuum, 2000), p. 26.

[33]Merton, *New Man*, p. 56.

Chapter 2: Longing

[1]Spanish phrase meaning "have a good pilgrimage."

[2]Mayberry is a fictional community in North Carolina that was the setting for the American television sitcom *The Andy Griffith Show*.

[3]I am not suggesting that being in relationship with children from around the world is the same as motherhood. For me, having no children of my own simply makes room for me to be available to children in poverty in different ways than if I had children of my own. More on this in the "Death" chapter.

[4]Christopher Webb taught me about longing at a Renovaré Conference in 2008 in Atlanta, Georgia—the last regional Renovaré conference with Dallas Willard and Richard Foster together.

[5]Hazel wood is chosen for its strong and flexible qualities.

[6]Chris and I are not tall by average standards. Instead of being referred to as short we prefer the term "fun size."

[7]Spanish for "companions."

[8]Macrina Wiederkehr, *Seven Sacred Pauses: Living Mindfully Through the Hours of the Day* (Notre Dame, Ind.: Sorin Books, 2008), p. 32.

[9]"Flight of the Bumblebee" is a well-known orchestral interlude written by Nikolai Rimsky-Korsakov for his opera *The Tale of Tsar Saltan*, composed in 1899-1900.

[10]"The Secret Life of Butterflies," *Studio 360*, NPR, KIOS 91.5, Omaha, Nebr. (December 8, 2007).

[11]Sue Monk Kidd, *When the Heart Waits: Spiritual Direction for Life's Sacred Questions* (New York: HarperCollins, 1990), p. 14.

[12]Augustine did a lot to preserve the gospel of Christ, even though he was imperfect and vulnerable to the worldview and limitations of his culture and society.

[13]Hebrews 11:1: "Now faith is being sure of what we hope for and certain of what we do not see" (NIV).

Chapter 3: Darkness

[1]We found out later that on this very day a pilgrim was hospitalized because of the intense climb and dangerous weather conditions, and a week earlier someone had actually died on this mountain pass.

[2]In St. John of the Cross, *Dark Night of the Soul: A Masterpiece in the Literature of Mysticism,* ed. E. Allison Peers (New York: Doubleday, 1959), p. 27.

[3]I highly recommend Fr. Richard Rohr's teaching on male spirituality.

[4]Kolkata is the present-day spelling of Calcutta, capital of West Bengal, India.

[5]For a summary of the Catholic (or Counter-) Reformation see Phyllis Tickle,

The Great Emergence (Grand Rapids: Baker, 2008), pp. 57-59.

[6]Lee Hoinacki, *El Camino: Walking to Santiago de Compostela* (University Park: Pennsylvania State University, 1996), p. 135.

[7]Kimberlee Conway Ireton, "The Gift of Darkness," *Relevant Magazine* online. The article has since been taken offline.

[8]Rob Bell notes these Scripture references in his Nooma film *She*, in which he explores the feminine attributes of God. Rob Bell, *She*, Nooma 021 (Grand Rapids: Flannel and Zondervan, 2008).

[9]St. John of the Cross, *Dark Night of the Soul*, p. 61.

[10]For further examination of the night of sense and night of spirit, see *Dark Night of the Soul* by St. John of the Cross or *Invitation to Love: The Way of Christian Contemplation* by Thomas Keating.

[11]St. John of the Cross, *Dark Night of the Soul*, p. 37.

[12]Ibid., p. 127.

[13]*The Cloud of Unknowing* is thought to have been written by an anonymous fourteenth-century English monk. The writing is strikingly similar to St. John of the Cross, who would likely not have been privy to *The Cloud* at the time of his writing *The Dark Night*.

[14]Cynthia Bourgeault, "From Woundedness to Union," *Gnosis*, Winter 1995, pp. 41-45.

[15]George MacDonald, *Unspoken Sermons* (Charleston, S.C.: BiblioBazaar, 2007), pp. 178-79.

Chapter 4: Death

[1]Kolkata is presumed to be named for Kali, the Hindu goddess of death and destruction.

[2]Joseph Langford, *Mother Teresa's Secret Fire* (Huntington, Ind.: Our Sunday Visitor, 2008), p. 92.

[3]Jon Sobrino, *The Principle of Mercy: Taking the Crucified People from the Cross* (Maryknoll, N.Y.: Orbis, 1994).

[4]W. Bader, ed., *Like a Drop in the Ocean: 99 Sayings by Mother Teresa* (Hyde Park, N.Y.: New City Press, 2006), n.p.

[5]Though Mother Teresa was Albanian by birth, she was granted Indian citizenship and was often mistaken for being Indian.

[6]Robert Kegan, *The Evolving Self* (Cambridge, Mass.: Harvard University Press, 1982). Kegan is a developmental psychologist and the William and Miriam Meehan Professor in Adult Learning and Professional Development at Harvard University.

[7]Henri Nouwen with Philip Roderick, *Beloved: Henri Nouwen in Conversation* (Grand Rapids: Eerdmans, 2007), p. 12.

[8]They did in fact go through with the marriage and have been a source of beautiful grace to one another.

[9]Carol Lakey Hess, *Caretakers of Our Common House: Women's Development in Communities of Faith* (Nashville: Abingdon, 1997), p. 66.

[10]Reginald F. Christian, ed., *Tolstoy's Letters*, vol. 2 (New York: Scribners, 1978), n.p.

[11]Ronald Rolheiser, *Forgotten Among the Lilies: Learning to Love Beyond Our Fears* (New York: Doubleday, 2004), p. 188. For a broader reflection on this content see Brian McLaren's *A New Kind of Christian* (San Francisco: Jossey-Bass, 2001). On pages x and xi he elaborates on this context of change. He includes a helpful diagram and explanation for the process, using different terminology but the same core idea.

[12]Cynthia Bourgeault, *Centering Prayer and Inner Awakening* (Cambridge, Mass.: Cowley, 2004), p. 49.

Chapter 5: Transformation

[1]Personal journal, October 5, 2007.

[2]A rule of life is generally associated with the monastic tradition for outlining a way of life to incorporate work, prayer and rest. In our contemporary times, rules of life help bring balance to these areas of the layperson's life.

[3]Tilden Edwards, *Sabbath Time* (Nashville: Upper Room Books, 2003), p. 63.

[4]Ibid., p. 79.

[5]Ibid., p. 73.

[6]Personal journal, November 23, 2007.

[7]The labyrinth prayer dates back to at least the twelfth century. Historically it was used by Christians in place of making pilgrimage to a holy site. The floor of Chartes Cathedral in France has a labyrinth that has been used by pilgrims for centuries. The labyrinth is a symbol for our spiritual journey. As we walk we journey toward the center, toward God. Throughout our movement we are interchangeably close to and far from the center. But even still, as we walk we are progressing closer to the center, no matter how far away we might seem. The labyrinth is a way to be fully present in the moment of our prayer. It is a prayer of embodiment: entering the labyrinth is embodying our inner desire to grow closer to God. Walk the labyrinth prayerfully. Let your walk be your prayer. As you walk, let your thoughts come and go with each step. The labyrinth can be a slow, quiet, meditative practice, though children often enjoy running or skipping in it. Walk as you so desire, but remain mindful of others in the labyrinth with you. You can search for a labyrinth near you on the Internet. Many churches and retreat centers make their labyrinth available to the public.

[8]Jackson's fundamental effort is Natural Systems Agriculture (NSA). NSA is rooted in the ideology that nature is comprised of perennial, symbiotic plants growing in a mixture. Being symbiotic means that two dissimilar organisms live together to the benefit of both. With the help of genetic biology Jackson has been breeding the grains we need to exist into perennials from the annuals humanity has created over a period of 10,000 years of agriculture. All plants started as perennials, and over many years, in order to create a larger seed head or yield per acre, we selected for the annual and gradually bred out the perennial qualities. For more information visit <www.landinstitute.org>.

[9]Mother Teresa, *Total Surrender* (Ann Arbor, Mich.: Servant, 1985), p. 107.

[10]Henri Nouwen, *Compassion* (New York: Doubleday, 1982), pp. 116-17. "Prayer and action, therefore, can never be seen as contradictory or mutually exclusive. Prayer without action grows in a powerless pietism, and action without prayer degenerates into questionable manipulation. If prayer leads us into a deeper unity with the compassionate Christ, it will always give rise to concrete acts of service. And if concrete acts of service do indeed lead us to a deeper solidarity with the poor, the hungry, the sick, the dying, and the oppressed, they will always give rise to prayer. In prayer we meet Christ, and in him all human suffering. In service we meet people, and in them the suffering Christ."

[11]Ibid.

[12]Parker Palmer, *The Active Life: A Spirituality of Work, Creativity and Caring* (San Francisco: Jossey-Bass, 1990), p. 39.

[13]Thomas Keating refers to God as the Divine Physician.

[14]Edwards, *Sabbath Time*, p. 76.

[15]Osha Gray Davidson, *The Best of Enemies: Race and Redemption in the New South* (Chapel Hill: University of North Carolina Press, 2001).

[16]*Lectio divina* is Latin for "sacred reading," though a more accurate definition might be "sacred listening." *Lectio divina* is a slow, contemplative praying of the Scriptures. Traditionally one progresses through the movements of *lectio* (reading/listening), *meditatio* (meditation), *oratio* (prayer) and finally *contemplatio* (contemplation). These traditional Latin movements are also associated in this manner: *lectio* (acquaintanceship), *meditatio* (friendly companionship), *oratio* (friendship), *contemplatio* (union). For more information I recommend M. Basil Pennington's book *Lectio Divina: Renewing the Ancient Practice of Praying the Scriptures*.

[17]Richard Rohr has an interesting perspective of God incarnating God's self as a man:

The "sacred feminine" is in many ways a rediscovery of Jesus' spirit, a reemergence of a well-suppressed truth, an eventual political upheaval, a certain reform of our hearing of the Gospel and someday perhaps the very structures of the churches—and all proceeding from a deep knowing in the feminine womb, the exact place from which we received Christ for the first time.

The feminist insight explains a vast majority of Jesus' teaching and style, a male acting very differently in an almost totally patriarchal Jewish society. Like Mary, the Church also has somehow "treasured these things in her heart" (Luke 2:19), but only in time will they be ready to come forth, like Jesus from her womb.

Jesus would never have broken through as a genuinely new revelation if he had acted nonviolently inside of a feminine body. It would not have been revolutionary or a challenge—because we expect and demand that women be patient, nurturing, forgiving, healing, self-effacing, and self-sacrificing. Women are expected to be nonviolent in a violent male society. But we are still not prepared for males or institutions or nations to act nonviolently, even in the church. That is why God had to become incarnate for us in the body of a man. Jesus had a male body but a very feminine soul, which was genuinely new. Unfortunately, we basically rejected most of Jesus' teachings and style as impractical and unreasonable in the pyramidal "real world" of church and state.

Adapted from Richard Rohr, *Simplicity: The Freedom of Letting Go* (New York: Crossroad, 2004), pp. 130-31.

Chapter 6: Intimacy

[1]Themes of abiding in God and loving one another are developed in John 15.

[2]William Johnston, ed., *The Cloud of Unknowing and The Book of Privy Counseling* (New York: Image Doubleday, 1973), p. 88.

[3]For a more detailed rendition of this story see Chris Heuertz, *Simple Spirituality: Learning to See God in a Broken World* (Downers Grove, Ill.: IVP Books, 2008), p. 141.

[4]For more exploration of cataphatic and apophatic prayer see Cynthia Bourgeault's book *Centering Prayer and Inner Awakening* (Cambridge, Mass.: Cowley, 2004), chap. 4.

[5]Kate Hurley, "Stronger Than Death," from her album *Sleeping When You Woke Me* (Worship Circle Records, 2006).

[6]Kahlil Gibran, *The Prophet* (New York: Alfred A. Knopf, 1923), pp. 11-15.

[7]Personal journal, September 23, 2007.

[8]Henri Nouwen, *Intimacy* (New York: HarperCollins), pp. 17-18.

[9]Richard J. Hauser, S.J., *Moving in the Spirit: Becoming a Contemplative in Action* (Mahwah, N.J.: Paulist, 1986), p. 25.

[10]Pelagius's teaching was condemned as heresy at numerous councils. Councils of Carthage (412, 416 and 418); Council of Ephesus (431); Council of Orange (529); Augsburg Confession (1530) Art. 9, 18 (Lutheran); Council of Trent (1546) (Roman Catholic); Gallican Confession (1559) Art. 10 (French Reformed); Belgic Confession (1561) Art. 15 (Lowlands, French/Dutch/German Reformed); Second Helvetic Confession (1561/1566) chaps. 8-9 (Swiss-German Reformed); Anglican Articles (1571) 9 (English); Canons of Dort (1618-1619) 3/4.2 (Dutch/German/French Reformed).

[11]Hauser, *Moving in the Spirit*, pp. 25-27.

[12]For a more in-depth discussion of the Western and Christian models of spirituality see chapter two of Hauser's *Moving in the Spirit*.

[13]Carla Mae Streeter, O.P., *Seasons of the Soul: An Intimate God in Liturgical Time* (St. Louis, Mo.: Chalice, 2004), p. 14.

Chapter 7: Union

[1]Personal journal, June 5, 2007.

[2]Lee Hoinacki, *El Camino: Walking to Santiago de Compostela* (University Park: Pennsylvania State University Press, 1996), p. 135.

[3]Richard J. Hauser, S.J., *Moving in the Spirit: Becoming a Contemplative in Action* (Mahwah, N.J.: Paulist, 1986), p. 13.

[4]Cynthia Bourgeault, *Centering Prayer and Inner Awakening* (Cambridge, Mass.: Cowley Publications, 2004), p. 93.

[5]"State or Way: Purgative, Illuminative, Unitive," *Catholic Encyclopedia* (accessed July 8, 2009) <www.newadvent.org/cathen/14254a.htm>.

[6]Elizabeth Gilbert, *Eat, Pray, Love* (New York: Viking, 2006), p. 274.

[7]Thomas Merton quoting Douglas Steere, Quaker theologian, in *Conjectures of a Guilty Bystander* (New York: Doubleday, 1968).

[8]Henri Nouwen, *Clowning in Rome* (New York: Random House, 2000), pp. 13-14.

[9]Ibid., p. 30.

[10]John Neafsey, *A Sacred Voice Is Calling: Personal Vocation and Social Conscience* (Maryknoll, N.Y.: Orbis, 2006), p. 1.

[11]John Main, *Word Made Flesh* (New York: Continuum, 1998), pp. 37-38.

[12]Frederick Buechner, *Wishful Thinking: A Seeker's ABC* (San Francisco: HarperSanFrancisco, 1993), p. 119. "The place God calls you to is the place where your deep gladness and the world's deep hunger meet."

Conclusion

[1]Parker Palmer, *The Active Life: A Spirituality of Work, Creativity and Caring* (San Francisco: Jossey-Bass, 1999), p. 39.

[2]Thomas Merton, "The Contemplative Life: Its Meaning and Necessity," *The Dublin Review* 223 (Winter 1949): 27.

[3]Austin Reparth, "At Home Again," in Pilgrim Cards (accessed June 10, 2009) <www.pilgrimcards.com/>.

ABOUT THE ARTIST

SARAH LANCE was born in 1973 in Los Angeles, California, and she studied fine art at the California State Polytechnic University in Pomona. Sarah's body of work has mainly been for personal spiritual and emotional process, and it has only been exhibited among close friends and family.

Sarah currently lives and works in Kolkata, India, as the director of Sari Bari, a business that employs women freed from the sex trade. Sari Bari is the primary expression of Sarah's artistic endeavors; she designs bags and quilts from recycled saris, restoring what has been cast off, in the hope that the lives of the women she serves will be made new.

Sarah is also the Word Made Flesh Asia regional coordinator, and she is a believer that the journey alongside those who are poor has been the most passionate, creative and artistic expression of her life.

LIKEWISE. *Go and do.*

A man comes across an ancient enemy, beaten and left for dead. He lifts the wounded man onto the back of a donkey and takes him to an inn to tend to the man's recovery. Jesus tells this story and instructs those who are listening to "go and do likewise."

Likewise books explore a compassionate, active faith lived out in real time. When we're skeptical about the status quo, Likewise books challenge us to create culture responsibly. When we're confused about who we are and what we're supposed to be doing, Likewise books help us listen for God's voice. When we're discouraged by the troubled world we've inherited, Likewise books encourage us to hold onto hope.

In this life we will face challenges that demand our response. Likewise books face those challenges with us so we can act on faith.

likewisebooks.com